RIGHT THROUGH THE PACK AGAIN

Right Through The Pack (A Bridge Fantasy) by Robert Darvas and Norman de V. Hart was published in 1948 and the idea of each card in the pack telling its own story was an instant hit. It is on virtually every magazine's and player's list of the top ten bridge books of all time and has become a bridge classic.

A series of articles by Ron Klinger appeared in *The Bridge World* magazine and featured the Old Master, who managed to snatch victory from impossible situations. Each of these articles is reproduced here. In the final article, Last Hurrah, the Old Master collapses and dies . . . or does he? In *Right Through The Pack Again* the cards strive to keep the Old Master alive. Each card tells its own tale and how it was the key feature. Not only will you be enchanted by the deals, but you will also learn more about why the Old Master has lost the zest for life. Will the cards be able to restore that zest?

Ron Klinger is a leading international bridge teacher and has represented Australia in many world championships from 1976 to 2007. He has written over fifty books, some of which have been translated into Bulgarian, Chinese, Danish, French, Hebrew and Icelandic. He has also written many articles for bridge magazines, including those featuring 'the Old Master', and has a website www.ronklingerbridge.com dedicated to the improvement of your game with daily problems and many weekly quizzes.

RIGHT THROUGH THE PACK AGAIN

Ron Klinger

Weidenfeld & Nicolson
IN ASSOCIATION WITH
PETER CRAWLEY

First published in Great Britain 2008
in association with Peter Crawley
by Weidenfeld & Nicolson
a division of the Orion Publishing Group Ltd
Orion House, 5 Upper St Martin's Lane, London WC2H 9EA

an Hachette Livre UK Company

The right of Ron Klinger to be identified as the author
of this book has been asserted by him in accordance
with the Copyright, Designs and Patents Act 1988

A catalogue record for this book
is available from the British Library

ISBN 978 0 297 84476 1

Typeset by Modern Bridge Publications
P.O. Box 140, Northbridge,
NSW 1560, Australia

Printed in Great Britain by
Clays Ltd, St Ives plc

The Orion Publishing Group's policy is to use papers that are natural, renewable
 and recyclable products and made from wood grown in sustainable forests.
The logging and manufacturing processes are expected to conform to the
 environmental regulations of the country of origin.

www.orionbooks.co.uk

CONTENTS

Introduction

At the end of a long tournament the Old Master collapses. He is at death's door and wants to go through. If he dies the pack of cards in his brain, in his soul, die with him. Their quest is to try to save the Old Master by recounting their favourite deals. They seek to restore a desire for life over death, to give him a reason for living whereas he feels he has lost it all.

That is the premise of *Right Through The Pack Again*, a pale sequel but a loving tribute to the original bridge classic, *Right Through The Pack*, by Robert Darvas and Norman de V. Hart, which was published in 1948. The original is among almost every bridge player's favourite books and deservedly appears regularly in lists of the top ten bridge books of all time.

The Old Master appeared first in the 1970s in *Last Board*, a bridge adaptation of the excellent chess article, *Last Round* by Kester Svendsen. Just as in Hollywood movies like *Rocky* and *Die Hard*, the Old Master strives to snatch victory from the jaws of almost inevitable defeat. The theme is best exemplified by these words from *Man of La Mancha*:

> *To dream the impossible dream*
> *To fight the unbeatable foe*
> *To bear the unbearable sorrow*
> *To run where the brave dare not go . . .*

> *And the world would be better for this*
> *That one man scorned and covered with scars*
> *Still strove with his last ounce of courage*
> *To reach the unreachable star*

That is the stuff of which the Old Master is made.

Just as the formula movies spawned sequels (how many *Rocky* movies or *Die Hards* have we had?), so every few years a new Old Master article appeared in *The Bridge World* magazine. You can read those early articles in Appendix 1: The Prequel. That will give you an insight into the Old Master's prowess.

Otherwise start with the Prologue, *Last Hurrah*, which takes you to where *Right Through The Pack Again* commences. You can always have a look at the prequel articles later.

When a book or movie is successful, sequels are commonplace as are remakes of movies or similar themes in books. It has been a surprise that it took so long for a second version of *Right Through The Pack* to appear. It did so in 2006 with the very clever and creative *Back Through The Pack* by Julian Pottage.

Just like Julian, I had been collecting deals for many years with the aim of producing a follow-up to *Right Through The Pack* and here it is. The deals come from lots of different areas, many from recent tournaments, some from rubber bridge and some were simply created. There is often a change of a card here and there to try to make deal foolproof and sometimes suits have been interchanged. You can find the source of all the deals in Appendix 2.

This is my quest, to follow that star . . .

I am sure you will enjoy the various quests of the Old Master and that of the pack of cards, who are trying to save him. I hope you will be moved to read the original and the Julian Pottage sequel, if you have not already done so.

Ron Klinger, 2008

THE CLUBS

THE DIAMONDS

THE HEARTS

THE SPADES

Prologue

Last Hurrah

© Bridge World Magazine Inc. 2001 (March issue)

Eight boards to go . . . the Bridgerama commentator's voice boomed through the packed stadium . . . *HELP leads by 76 Imps and will be the Champion yet again . . . the human team has done well, but humans can no longer compete against the bridge computers . . even the Old Master is no match for their speed and skill . . . the latest Bermuda Bowl as good as over . . .*

The Old Master sat in his slightly darkened room. He stared at his screen, waiting for the next hand to appear. Eight boards left. 70 Imps behind when the session began. None of the early boards in the final session offered hope of significant gain. It seemed as though H.E.L.P., the Highest Expert Level Player computer, would sweep all before it once more. World champion for the past five years, HELP was on the verge of annexing its next title.

Still, they had done well to reach the final. Humans had not played in a final for the past four years. World championships had become a battle between the top programs and HELP had proved itself the best. The public lost interest in the battles between computers and had given the human teams no chance even when they won the national and zonal rounds.

Zonal winners competed against each other in long knockout matches. With the advent of computer domination, the world championships were no longer held in one location. Computers did not tire and did not suffer jet-lag. All late stage matches were played via the 'net. Computer programs were vetted to ensure there was no possibility of 'peeking' and each human competitor had two human monitors (from different continents) in the same room to ensure no illegal communication.

When one of the finalists turned out to be a team of humans, it made front page news. Worldwide publicity led to the match being broadcast live and, seeing another avenue for profit, entrepreneurs hailed it as the match of the millenium.

Theatres, entertainment centres, stadiums around the world were booked out. Giant screens and expert commentators kept the public entertained, thanks in part to the computer commentator, a voice-generating version of HELP, to explain the bidding and play of the HELP 'players'.

The Old Master started to drift. The memory of his family flitted across his mind. When thirteen cards flashed on to his screen, he returned to reality.

♠ A 6 3
♡ 5
♢ A J 10 6 4
♣ A K Q 9

His partner was dealer, East-West were vulnerable. 1♡ from North, pass. He bid 2♢. Pause. The next three calls were always transmitted with equal time spacing between each. Pass, 2♡ from North, Pass. He rebid 3♣. Another pause. Pass, 3♠ from North, Pass. Fourth suit. He had to make an effort for slam but what was best? He made up his mind. 5NT. Pause. Pass, 6♢, Pass. He passed and waited for the opening lead. It was the ♠7.

WEST	NORTH	EAST	SOUTH
	1♡	Pass	2♢
Pass	2♡	Pass	3♣
Pass	3♠	Pass	5NT
Pass	6♢	All pass	

In the closed room HELP also reached six diamonds . . . said the Bridgerama commentator, as he revealed complete deal to the packed crowd.

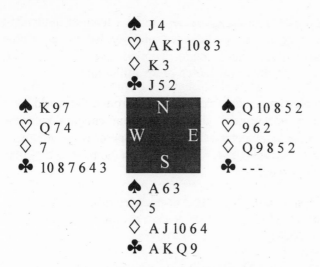

♠ J 4
♡ A K J 10 8 3
◇ K 3
♣ J 5 2

♠ K 9 7
♡ Q 7 4
◇ 7
♣ 10 8 7 6 4 3

♠ Q 10 8 5 2
♡ 9 6 2
◇ Q 9 8 5 2
♣ - - -

♠ A 6 3
♡ 5
◇ A J 10 6 4
♣ A K Q 9

After 1 ♡, 2 ◇, 2 ♡, 3 ♣, HELP North bid 3 ◇ and HELP South stopped in 6 ◇ after finding the ◇Q was missing.

'Yes, we had better auction,' interjected HELP.

But you didn't make it, said the commentator.

'South took good line. Won spade lead, cashed ♡A, ♡K, no ♡Q dropped, heart ruff and they were 3-3. Now ◇K and diamond finesse. That worked but with the diamonds 5-1 and clubs 5-0, slam doomed from the start.'

On the ♣7 lead the Old Master played the jack from dummy, covered by the ♠Q, taken with the ace. He considered his choices. 'If I take the heart finesse and it loses, that is the end. I can pitch a spade on the second heart at once but I have another spade loser. I'll have to play the diamonds some time. Why not now?'

He played a low diamond to the king and continued with the ◇3 to his jack. When West showed out The Old Master leaned back in his chair. 'Now I will have to take the heart finesse,' he thought. 'I cannot afford to try to ruff the hearts good.'

A heart to the jack held and then came the $\heartsuit$A and $\heartsuit$K, declarer discarding spades. 'Should I cash one club now, before continuing the hearts?' he thought.

He saw there was no need for that and simply played the hearts. If East ruffed, South would over-ruff, cash the top diamond and play clubs. East discarded three spades on the hearts, while declarer threw club winners. The Old Master then led dummy's spade and ruffed with the $\diamondsuit$6. He exited with the $\clubsuit$A and claimed twelve tricks.

Perfectly timed . . . Old Master has lost none of his spark . . . Seven years since he last played at this level but still retains his brilliance . . . 14 imps to the Challengers . . . still trail by 62 . . . here is the next deal . . .

With both sides vulnerable on the next deal, East passed and the Old Master opened 1NT on:

$\spadesuit$ A K 2
$\heartsuit$ Q 9 8 4
$\diamondsuit$ K Q 5
$\clubsuit$ K 7 6

Two hearts from West. . . 'Buzz'. In addition to the warning sound, a Red Alert message started flashing on the screen. He pressed the E button for Explanation.

'Transfer to spades' appeared on the screen.

3$\clubsuit$ from North, Pass from East.

'3$\clubsuit$ is forcing, but I am not really worth a raise,' he thought. He bid 3NT.

Pause. 4$\heartsuit$ on his left, 4$\spadesuit$ from partner, Pass.

'What does 4$\spadesuit$ mean?' he thought. 'Not a control bid. No, partner wants me to choose the contract.'

He bid 4NT and everyone passed. The lead was the ♡A and dummy appeared on his screen. Around the stadium, the North-South cards appeared on the giant screens. Beneath each screen was a constant flow of advertising, mostly for ICU (International Cyber Utilities), the company which created HELP.

♠ Q 8 5
♡ 3
◇ A J 10 2
♣ A J 9 8 4

♠ A K 2
♡ Q 9 8 4
◇ K Q 5
♣ K 7 6

'We have 29 high card points and yet West bid on to 4♡,' thought the Old Master. 'Obviously he is very shapely.'

The Old Master still thought of the opponents in human terms. It did not occur to him to refer to his opponent as 'it'.

East played the ♡6 on the ♡A and West switched to the ♠J at trick 2.

'Nine tricks are there, but where is the tenth? It is hardly likely that West with such length in the majors will have the ♣Q. Maybe we can find out.'

The Old Master cashed the ♣K and West discarded a spade.

'That ends that chance,' he thought. 'What do I do now?'

In the stadium the commentator had revealed the complete deal to the audience:

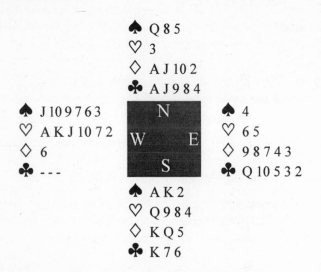

♠ Q 8 5
♡ 3
◇ A J 10 2
♣ A J 9 8 4

♠ J 10 9 7 6 3
♡ A K J 10 7 2
◇ 6
♣ - - -

♠ 4
♡ 6 5
◇ 9 8 7 4 3
♣ Q 10 5 3 2

♠ A K 2
♡ Q 9 8 4
◇ K Q 5
♣ K 7 6

In the closed room, reported the commentator, West jumped to 4♡ over 1NT. North doubled for takeout and South left it in. With no inkling of West's second suit, North led the ♠5. South took the king and switched to a trump. Declarer finessed the jack and ruffed a spade in dummy. After a club ruff to hand, West cashed the ♡A and ♡K, then conceded a spade. When the spades broke 3-3, he lost just two spades, a heart and a diamond. One down, +200 to HELP.

'Good bid by West,' conceded HELP, grudgingly it seemed. 'But HELP did the right thing by playing 4♡ doubled. 5♣ is a disaster and the best the Old Master can do is take his nine tricks. As soon as East comes in with the ♣Q, a heart back will defeat 4NT. HELP will win another 100 and 7 Imps here.'

The crowd waited expectantly. They could see that 4NT would fail, but still they hoped for some magic, some rabbit from the Old Master's hat. They did not have long to wait.

At trick 4 the Old Master led the ♡9.

'What's this?' went a shout.

'He's gone mad.'

'No, wait.'

West won the ♡9 with the ten and East followed with the ♡5. West now paused for quite some time, a rarity for these speed machines.

He's going to make it, folks, the commentator shrieked, *If West cashes the ♡A, the ♡Q will be declarer's tenth trick . . . if he doesn't, East has no heart later to come back to West.*

Before the commentator could finish his analysis, the play unfolded. West exited with the ♠10 and the Old Master cashed three rounds of diamonds, coming down to this position:

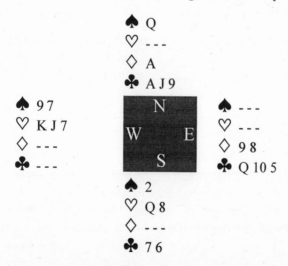

Next came the ♠Q and East was in trouble. If he threw a club, the Old Master would play ace and another club. He therefore discarded a diamond. The Old Master cashed the ◇A and now exited with the ♣9. East won, but dummy had the last two tricks.

7 imps to HELP, was it?' chided the commentator, *I don't think so. How about 9 imps to the Challengers? They trail by 53. And we have some excitement on the next deal, ladies and gentlemen.*

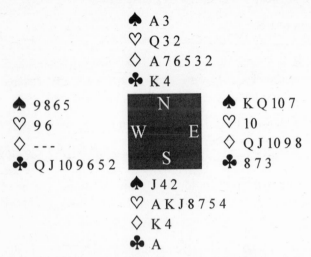

♠ A 3
♡ Q 3 2
♢ A 7 6 5 3 2
♣ K 4

♠ 9 8 6 5
♡ 9 6
♢ - - -
♣ Q J 10 9 6 5 2

♠ K Q 10 7
♡ 10
♢ Q J 10 9 8
♣ 8 7 3

♠ J 4 2
♡ A K J 8 7 5 4
♢ K 4
♣ A

The commentator broke into an excited jabber: *HELP bid to 7 ♡, an excellent contract. Normally you would expect to have no problems. Draw trumps, set up the diamonds . . . The ♣Q was led and HELP cashed the ♡A, ♡K, leaving the ♡Q as an entry to dummy . . . when the diamonds were 5-0, the grand slam was one down. Let's hope the Challengers stop in a lower contract.'*

The Old Master was the dealer, neither side vulnerable. He opened 1♡. 3♣ on his left, 4♣ from partner, Pass. He pressed E. 'Which call?' prompted the computer. '3♣' he typed. 'Weak jump-overcall' came the reply. 'Press E again for expanded explanation.' He didn't bother.

His partner's 4♣ was a strong raise in hearts and so he bid 4NT. Roman Key Card was standard nowadays. Pass, 5♠, Pass.

'Two key cards plus the ♡Q,' he thought. 'What else?' He bid 5NT, asking for kings. Pass, 6♢, Pass. The crowd began their chant. 'Six hearts, six hearts, six hearts. . .'

'One outside king,' thought the Old Master. 'No doubt HELP will reach 6♡. We are so far behind, no point being timid.'

'Six hearts, six hearts . . .' It rose to a crescendo.

He bid seven hearts.

Silence.

The lead was the ♣Q. He won with the ace and drew trumps, ♡A, then ♡J. Next came the ◇K, the bad news revealed.

'Only one hope now,' he thought.

He continued with a spade to the ace, cashed the ♣K, discarding a spade and then led the ♡Q, overtaking with the ♡K. Three more rounds of hearts left:

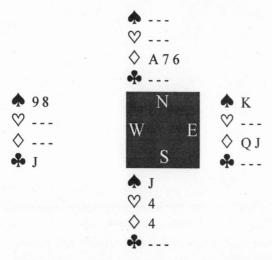

The Old Master led his last trump and East could not guard both spades and diamonds. When East discarded the ♠K, South claimed the last two tricks.

The crowd rose and cheered.

+1510 to the Challengers. +17 imps.

They shouted and clapped.

Challengers still trail by 36 Imps.

The crowd fell silent.

The public is really behind the human Challengers . . .

'Yes,' said HELP, 'we have a term for that . . . emotion sickness.'

The next deal appeared:

♠ K 10 8 7 3
♡ K J 5
◇ 8 3
♣ K 6 2

♠ A 9 5
♡ A 6 2
◇ K J 10 7
♣ A 4 3

With only North-South vulnerable, West and North passed. East opened 2◇. 'Buzz'. Red Alert. The Old Master pressed the E button. 'Multi, weak two in either major.' He bid 2NT. Pass, 3♡ from North, Pass. The Old Master pressed the alert button. The computers rarely sought explanations, but the alerts were still compulsory. He accepted the transfer with 3♠. Pass, 3NT, Pass. He removed to 4♠, passed out. The opening lead was the ♡7.

'3NT would have been much easier,' he thought, 'especially with North having such good hearts. Anyway, what are we to do here?' As there was no point in playing dummy's jack, the Old Master played low from dummy and captured East's eight with the ace. He clicked on the ♠A: four – three – queen.

'What now?' he wondered.

In the meantime the commentator had revealed the complete deal and described what had happened at the other table:

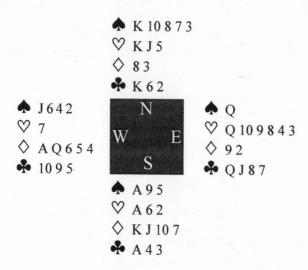

```
                    ♠ K 10 8 7 3
                    ♡ K J 5
                    ◇ 8 3
                    ♣ K 6 2
    ♠ J 6 4 2                         ♠ Q
    ♡ 7                               ♡ Q 10 9 8 4 3
    ◇ A Q 6 5 4                       ◇ 9 2
    ♣ 10 9 5                          ♣ Q J 8 7
                    ♠ A 9 5
                    ♡ A 6 2
                    ◇ K J 10 7
                    ♣ A 4 3
```

The bidding went the same way and the lead was the ♡7. Declarer won the ace, cashed the ♠A and ran the ♠9 next. After another spade finesse, the last trump was drawn, South throwing a club. A diamond to the jack was allowed to hold. After a club to the king another diamond was played. West won and exited with a club. Declarer made ten tricks with five spades, two hearts, one diamond and two clubs. The Old Master should find the same line and make the same number of tricks . . .

'Yes,' added HELP, 'even humans know about restricted choice. Simple mathematics.'

'The percentage play is to take the spade finesse,' thought the Old Master, 'but if East wins and returns a heart, West will ruff. Then there might be two losers in diamonds.'

While the Old Master was thinking, the crowd became restless.

'Why doesn't he play?'

'What is he thinking about?'

'It's obvious to finesse.'

Someone called out 'Finesse the spade. Finesse the spade.' Again the crowd took it up and the roar was soon deafening.

The Old Master made up his mind. He led the ♠5 and when West followed with the ♠2 he went up with the ♠K.

A groan ran round the crowd.

'Ah, a human moment,' said HELP.

The Old Master continued with the ♢8: nine – jack – four.

'Good defence by West,' said HELP. 'With only one entry left to the South hand, ducking the diamond holds declarer to one diamond trick.'

'They found the same duck at the other table,' said the commentator.

'Ah, yes. Humans can find such plays occasionally,' replied HELP. 'Random factor.'

'The Old Master is now destined to lose one trick in each suit and go one down,' said the commentator, *'That will be 12 Imps to HELP.'*

The Old Master continued with the ♠9, taken by the jack. West shifted to the ♣10, taken by the king and the ♠10 drew West's last trump. Dummy's diamond was played and South's ♢7 lost to the queen.

When West exited with the ♣5, the Old Master won in hand. These were the cards still lit up on all the screens:

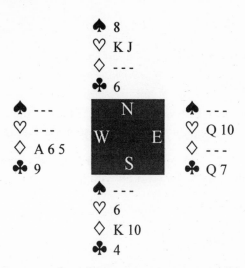

♠ 8
♡ K J
◇ - - -
♣ 6

♠ - - -
♡ - - -
◇ A 6 5
♣ 9

♠ - - -
♡ Q 10
◇ - - -
♣ Q 7

♠ - - -
♡ 6
◇ K 10
♣ 4

The ◇K was led, covered by the ace and ruffed in dummy. East could not afford to discard another heart and so let go a club. The Old Master now played dummy's club, not caring which defender took it. If East, a heart would go into dummy's tenace, if West a diamond return would give South the diamond trick plus a heart back to dummy.

No swing, no swing, shouted the commentator. *The Old Master has squared the board. Great play, even though in a lost cause. Only 4 boards to go . . . HELP still leads by 36 . . .*

The Old Master waited for the cards to appear. Were the last few boards pickups or were they pushes? Was there a chance or was the margin too great? The spectators would know, the players could only speculate.

Suddenly he felt a heavy weariness. As he sank into his chair, a searing flash and a vision filled his head. His wife and children again. His son, killed in that terrible car accident. His daughter, much too young, dead from a stroke, leaving behind a husband and three children. The pain flooded through him.

He missed them so. How could he go on without them? For so
many years he had lost the desire to live. There was no joy. Only
his love for bridge saved him from disintegration, but still he
longed for the release of death. He wished only to join them once
more. His one fear, that there was no hereafter, no chance of
reunion, no hope to see his beloved ones again.

His cards flashed on to the screen. With both sides vulnerable,
North and East had passed.

♠ Q
♡ A K J 5
◇ A 10 6 2
♣ Q 10 8 2

He opened 1◇. On his left, 2♠. Double from partner, 3♠ on
the right. He hit E. '2♠ is a weak jump-overcall.'

'Too late in the day to be delicate,' he thought. He bid 4♡. All
passed and the ♠A was led.

♠ J 7
♡ Q 10 8 3 2
◇ K 9 7 3
♣ 5 4

♠ Q
♡ A K J 5
◇ A 10 6 2
♣ Q 10 8 2

He ruffed the second spade and drew trumps in two rounds.

'Without a lucky layout in diamonds, there will be a diamond loser, as well as a spade and two clubs. How can I deal with this?'

The commentator had displayed the complete deal:

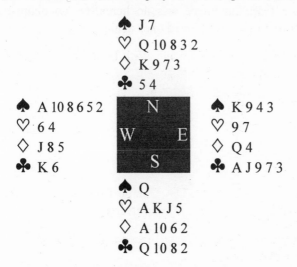

```
              ♠ J 7
              ♡ Q 10 8 3 2
              ◇ K 9 7 3
              ♣ 5 4
♠ A 10 8 6 5 2                    ♠ K 9 4 3
♡ 6 4                            ♡ 9 7
◇ J 8 5                          ◇ Q 4
♣ K 6                            ♣ A J 9 7 3
              ♠ Q
              ♡ A K J 5
              ◇ A 10 6 2
              ♣ Q 10 8 2
```

In the closed room, HELP South opened 1◇, West bid 2♠, North doubled and East jumped to 4♠. South doubled and everyone passed. Declarer lost the first four tricks and was one down. +200 to HELP.

Good judgment by North-South, added HELP.

Yes. With a diamond to lose and three inevitable black losers, the Old Master will be one down.

The crowd waited. They could see the losers. How could the Old Master deal with them? They had not long to wait. After ruffing the second spade, followed by ♡A and the ♡5 to dummy's ten, the Old Master led the ♣5.

'If I had ♣Q-10-9-2, I would have a chance,' he thought. 'These clubs are almost as good.'

When East played low, he put in the ♣8. West won with the king and, reluctant to open up the diamonds, returned the ♣6. East took the ace, but was stuck. Another club would allow declarer to finesse the ten and have two winners to discard diamonds. East shifted to the ◇Q, but the Old Master had made up his mind. He rose with the ace and led the ◇10, running it when West played low. Ten tricks were there.

Another piece of magic. You're seeing it all today. +620 and 9 more imps to the Challengers. 3 boards left . . . HELP leads by 27.

Neither vulnerable. East opened 3♡. The Old Master looked at:

> ♠ A Q J 10 9 8
> ♡ K Q 3
> ◇ A Q 9 7
> ♣ - - -

'Too good for 3♠. Even 4♠ does not do this justice. 5♠? Looks too much if partner has nothing.' He doubled. Pass, 5♣, Pass.

'I guess I had that coming.' He bid 5♠. Pass, 6♠, Double on his right. Everyone passed and after a little time, West led the ♣J.

> ♠ K
> ♡ 10 6 2
> ◇ 10 8 6 2
> ♣ A K Q 9 7

> ♠ A Q J 10 9 8
> ♡ K Q 3
> ◇ A Q 9 7
> ♣ - - -

'Typical human bidding,' commented HELP to the crowd. 'Bewilderness adventure.'

The Old Master played the ♣A. East followed with the ♣2.

'What do I discard?' he wondered. 'What was East's double? Asking for an unusual lead. So? I see, East must be void in diamonds. That gives West the five missing diamonds. If I throw three hearts on the clubs, I will lose two diamonds later. If I throw three diamonds, I will lose two hearts later.'

Still he did not play from hand. Working with his thesis as to how the red suits were divided he pictured the cards in a position five tricks ahead. Yes, the plan was fine . . .

Meanwhile the crowd had seen the whole deal. It was as the Old Master expected.

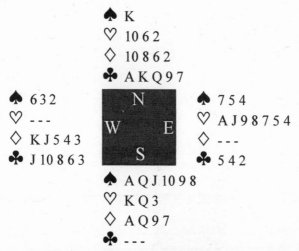

```
              ♠ K
              ♡ 10 6 2
              ♢ 10 8 6 2
              ♣ A K Q 9 7
 ♠ 6 3 2          N          ♠ 7 5 4
 ♡ - - -                     ♡ A J 9 8 7 5 4
 ♢ K J 5 4 3   W     E       ♢ - - -
 ♣ J 10 8 6 3                ♣ 5 4 2
                   S
              ♠ A Q J 10 9 8
              ♡ K Q 3
              ♢ A Q 9 7
              ♣ - - -
```

In the closed room, East opened 3♡ and South bid 4♠ passed out. West led the ♣J and declarer discarded the three heart losers on the clubs. At the end there were two diamond losers, +650 to HELP. Luckily for declarer a diamond was not led. That would allow a defensive cross-ruff for the first three tricks and +300 to East-West . . .

'You mean lucky for the Old Master,' interjected HELP. 'If West had led a diamond against 6♠ doubled, that would be +1400 to East-West . . . Still, +13 Imps to us will be adequate reward for sensible bidding.'

The Old Master completed his play to trick 1. On the ♣A he discarded the ♢Q. There was a collective gasp from the crowd.

'What?'

'Must be fatigue.'

'Getting too old.'

They had not seen what the Old Master saw.

At trick 2 he led the ♠K and overtook it with his ace.

'He's left the club winners in dummy.'

'He's mad.'

'Poor chap. He's lost it.'

He drew trumps in two more rounds, discarding a diamond and a club from dummy. Next came the ♡K. East ran through all the combinations. The newest versions of HELP could calculate 5,000 positions a second. East played low on the ♡K.

As East had only hearts and clubs left, the commentator explained, *to take the ♡A would leave East end-played. A heart return would allow declarer to win with dummy's ten and a club return would give declarer three more club tricks to throw a heart and two more diamonds. East has done well . . . Hang on, he's going to make the slam . . . he's . . .*

The crowd watched, mesmerized as they saw this ending:

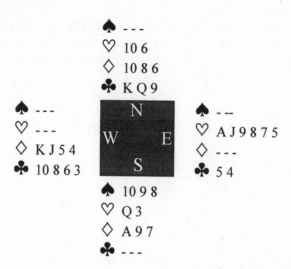

♠ - - -
♡ 10 6
♢ 10 8 6
♣ K Q 9

♠ - - -
♡ - - -
♢ K J 5 4
♣ 10 8 6 3

♠ - - -
♡ A J 9 8 7 5
♢ - - -
♣ 5 4

♠ 10 9 8
♡ Q 3
♢ A 9 7
♣ - - -

With a heart trick in, the Old Master shifted to a low diamond. If West played low, dummy would overtake and reach the stranded clubs. West won with the ♢J. A diamond return would surrender and West returned the ♣8, but the Old Master inserted the ♣9. The slam was home.

Unbelievable . . . simply unbelievable . . . have you seen anything like this? . . . +1430 . . . + 13 imps to the Challengers . . . they trail by just 14 Imps . . . we have a contest . . .

The crowd hooted. They stomped. Even the nerds who had come to see their favourite computers thrash the opposition were on their feet and cheering.

When some order had been restored, the next deal appeared. The crowd was despondent. The Old Master had an almost worthless hand.

Dealer South : North-South vulnerable

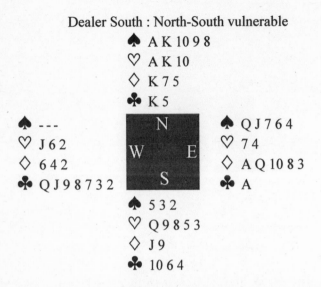

♠ A K 10 9 8
♡ A K 10
♢ K 7 5
♣ K 5

♠ ---
♡ J 6 2
♢ 6 4 2
♣ Q J 9 8 7 3 2

♠ Q J 7 6 4
♡ 7 4
♢ A Q 10 8 3
♣ A

♠ 5 3 2
♡ Q 9 8 5 3
♢ J 9
♣ 10 6 4

In the closed room, South passed and West opened 3♣, certainly reasonable at this vulnerability. North bid 4♠, East doubled and everyone passed. East led the ♣A, followed by a switch to the ♡7. North won, cashed the ♠A, ♠K and led the ♠10. East won and played another heart to North who continued with the ♠9. East took it and returned a trump. North won and discarded two diamonds on dummy's hearts but there was still a diamond to lose. One down. +200 to the Challengers. Let's see what happens in the open room . . .

The Old Master passed, West opened 3♣ and North thought for some time, then Double. Pass from East, 3♡ from the Old Master. Pass from West. Again North thought for some time. Then 4♡ from North.

A cheer reverberated around the stadium. With the Old Master at the helm, hope was there.

Don't get too excited, warned the commentator, *Declarer could lose two clubs, two diamonds and a spade. No swing. At best 4 ♡ will be one down . . . Remember the Old Master is only human . . .*

'Better than human. Plays almost as well as a computer,' added HELP.

The ♣Q was led. Someone shouted, 'Play low', but before the crowd could join in, the Old Master had played low and East won with the ace. The trump return was won with dummy's ace, followed by the ♡K and South won the third heart. Next came a low spade. When West showed out, the ♠10 was inserted and East won with the jack. Unwilling to give dummy a diamond trick, East returned a low spade.

Dummy's ♠8 won and the Old Master then cashed the ♠A and ♠K, discarding a diamond. Then came dummy's last spade. East played the ♠Q and South ditched his last diamond. East led the ♢A, South ruffed and a club to dummy allowed declarer to discard his club loser on the ♢K. Ten tricks made.

Another incredible result . . . +620 to the Challengers . . . another 13 imps . . . the Challengers are 1 Imp behind . . . can you believe this . . . one board left . . . will there be one more miracle?

The pain in the Old Master's head increased. He did not know what was wrong. A part of his mind still held the vision of his lost family. He wrapped his hands around his head, waiting.

The last deal is an easy partial, announced the commentator, displaying the full deal:

Dealer West : East-West vulnerable

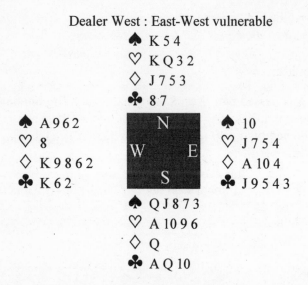

- ♠ K 5 4
- ♡ K Q 3 2
- ◇ J 7 5 3
- ♣ 8 7

West:
- ♠ A 9 6 2
- ♡ 8
- ◇ K 9 8 6 2
- ♣ K 6 2

East:
- ♠ 10
- ♡ J 7 5 4
- ◇ A 10 4
- ♣ J 9 5 4 3

South:
- ♠ Q J 8 7 3
- ♡ A 10 9 6
- ◇ Q
- ♣ A Q 10

In the closed room South opened 1 ♠ in fourth seat. North raised to 2 ♠ and everyone passed. West led the ◇6. East won with the ace and returned the ◇10. Declarer discarded a club and West won. Declarer lost two trump tricks but made the rest for +140. Top result for HELP. The Challengers cannot gain unless they reach game and make it, but game is doomed . . . valiant performance by the Challengers . . . so close and yet so far . . .

As in the other room, the auction started with three passes. The Old Master opened 1♠. Pass, 2♠, Pass. He perused his cards.

'He will pass.'

'No, he'll make a move.'

'So what? Game isn't on.'

The crowd was working itself to a frenzy, ready to erupt if the Old Master bid the game. Still he thought, but it was not about his cards. The shades of his family had become stronger still. They almost filled his mind. With an effort he pulled himself back to the last hand.

'Three hearts,' he bid, inviting game. Pass, 4♡, Pass.

'No.'

'Oh, no. Not hearts.'

When 4♡ was passed out, West knew what to do. The bidding made it obvious that East was short in spades and so West started with ♠A followed by the ♠2. The king was played from dummy and East ruffed.

The two of spades has asked for a club return. West could have played the ♠9 to ask for a diamond return or the ♠6 as an ambivalent signal, but the ♠2 was certainly reasonable. I predict East will shift to a club.

His words had hardly ended when the ♣4 hit the table. The Old Master considered his choices. He tried to focus though his eyes were growing dimmer.

If East had started with three hearts, the contract would succeed. The bad break means that 4 ♡ will fail . . . If the Old Master finesses, that is instant doom. I'm sure the ♣A will be played, but when trumps are drawn, and he has to draw them, he can discard one club and one diamond from dummy, but dummy will have only one trump left . . .

'Even the Old Master cannot ruff two losers with one trump,' added HELP.

The play of the ♣A drew muted cheers from the crowd. After removing the missing trumps, he cashed the ♠Q, then the ♠J discarding a club from dummy.

His sight was almost gone even though there was a glowing brightness in his mind. He could see his children in their infancy, their birthdays, the anniversaries. He could just make out the image on his screen.

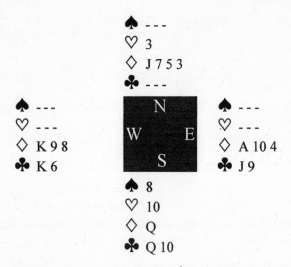

♠ - - -
♡ 3
◇ J 7 5 3
♣ - - -

♠ - - -
♡ - - -
◇ K 9 8
♣ K 6

♠ - - -
♡ - - -
◇ A 10 4
♣ J 9

♠ 8
♡ 10
◇ Q
♣ Q 10

The Old Master played the ♠8. He had already envisaged the ending. 'Neither can reduce to a singleton club,' he thought, 'else I can drop the king or pin the jack. They will have to discard a diamond each.'

West took some time, then threw a diamond, as did dummy and East. The Old Master picked over the position lovingly. One trick needed from the minors, but both minors guarded by both opponents. Each had a key honour in each minor, yet no matter which opponent won the next trick and no matter which minor they chose they would have to yield the critical trick.

Suddenly the brightness filled his mind. He saw his family clearly. There was warmth, there was love, they beckoned him. Tears of joy rolled down his cheeks. 'At last,' he thought, and as he slipped away to join them, he played the ◇Q and typed just one word on the keyboard:

'Checkmate.'

[*Last Hurrah* appeared in *The Bridge World* magazine in March, 2001. Subscriptions are available from the www.bridgeworld.com website.]

. . . now read on . . .

Right Through The Pack Again

The ambulance was there in minutes. The paramedics placed the Old Master on the stretcher, wheeled it to the ambulance and lifted him in. Seconds later, siren blaring, it raced to the hospital.

"He has a pulse, but it is very weak."

"His face is as ashen as any I've seen. I doubt he'll make it."

They were at the hospital. They wheeled the stretcher into Emergency with a great sense of urgency.

"Cardiac arrest," shouted one of the paramedics.

The operation went well, according to the lead doctor, as they moved the Old Master into Intensive Care, but the Old Master remained in a coma.

Days passed and the Old Master was still in a coma.

"I don't understand it," said the head doctor. "He should be out of it by now."

"I think he does not want to come out of it," said his colleague, the Australian expert on coma patients. "He is not displaying any will to live. He is getting weaker all the time. If he refuses to muster any strength, he will not last long. Gradually the organs will shut down. What he needs is a reason to keep on living."

The doctor's news was relayed quickly by the 10 of diamonds, who was on watch duty, to the king of spades. Immediately the spade king called a meeting of all the cards in the pack, not just the organizing kings and the supporting queens, but also the aces, the consultants who were there purely to give advice.

The dread news spread quickly through the pack, as they hastened to the meeting. The spade king repeated the grave situation.

"It looks as thought the Old Master will die soon. When he dies, we all die, too."

"I don't want to die," wailed the two of hearts.

"I don't either," cried the heart three.

The heart queen held the heart two by the hand and the heart three in the other.

"Hush, little ones," she said. "We will not die."

"Face reality," said the spade ace sternly.

"But the Old Master loves us so much."

"He loved his family even more and you know what happened to them. Just remember that we are all figcards of his imagination. When he dies, so do all of us."

"But he might be reborn," chipped in the six of clubs.

"Perhaps, but that will be without us. If and when he is reborn, we will no longer be with him. His mental slate will be wiped clean."

"I don't want to die." The two of hearts was off again and the others twos started crying as well.

"If we are to survive," said the queen of diamonds, "then we must keep the Old Master alive."

"How can we do that? You heard the doctors' report how weak he has become."

"If we can keep his mind alive, the mind will work on the rest of his body. If the mind dies, so will the Old Master and so will we. If the mind stays alive, we can survive."

"Easy to say," said the club eight, "but what can we do to keep his mind alive?"

"What if we try to remember a special occasion where each one of us had an important role to play?" said the diamond ace. "If we can show the Old Master how important he made each of us feel, that will let him know how important he is to us."

"An excellent idea," responded the club ace. "Let's get to work. Think of your good times, your best moment, your personal special deal."

"That's easy for me," said the spade four. "Can I go first?"

Up for promotion

The story of the ♠4

"It was an international Open Teams event, and I was the lowest card in the Old Master's hand," said the ♠4, "but that did not make me any the less valuable in the outcome."

Dealer North : Nil vulnerable

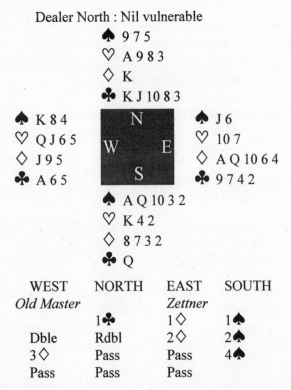

```
              ♠ 9 7 5
              ♡ A 9 8 3
              ◇ K
              ♣ K J 10 8 3
♠ K 8 4                        ♠ J 6
♡ Q J 6 5         N            ♡ 10 7
◇ J 9 5       W       E        ◇ A Q 10 6 4
♣ A 6 5           S            ♣ 9 7 4 2
              ♠ A Q 10 3 2
              ♡ K 4 2
              ◇ 8 7 3 2
              ♣ Q
```

WEST	NORTH	EAST	SOUTH
Old Master		*Zettner*	
	1♣	1◇	1♠
Dble	Rdbl	2◇	2♠
3◇	Pass	Pass	4♠
Pass	Pass	Pass	

The Old Master led the ◇5 to the king and ace and East switched to the ♡10, won by South. The ♣Q came next. The Old Master took the ace and continued with the ♡Q. Declarer covered with dummy's ♡A and cashed the ♣K and ♣J, on which he discarded a heart and a diamond.

Declarer had already lost two tricks and could not risk a fourth club. He switched to the ♡8 and Zettner ruffed in with the ♠J. Declarer over-ruffed with the ♠Q. To my surprise the Old Master followed with the ♡J, keeping the ♡6 and leaving the ♡9 high in dummy. This was now the position:

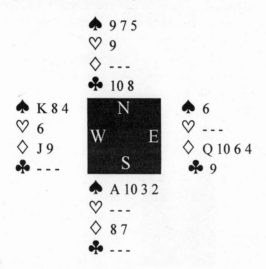

Declarer ruffed a diamond in dummy and called for the ♡9. East ruffed with the ♠6, over-ruffed by the ♠10. South's last diamond was ruffed with the ♠7 and the ♠9 was played next.

When East showed out, declarer played low and the Old Master won with the ♠K. He returned the ♠8 to declarer's ace, concluded the spade four, but I was the one to take care of declarer's ♠3 at trick 13. Has anyone seen a defender win trick 13 with the four of trumps or lower?

That's all very well, said the nine of spades, but you would not be so cocky if declarer had played it better. After South over-ruffed the ♠J with the ♠Q, I was sending out messages to the ♠2 and ♠3. Push yourselves forward, I willed them. If declarer plays one of you next he will be all right.

Either my mental telepathy is not good enough or the lowest spades are not strong enough to make their presence felt. Anyway, said the spade nine, I was able to help the Old Master in quite a similar way . . .

Unkindest cut

The story of the ♠9

South dealer : Nil vulnerable

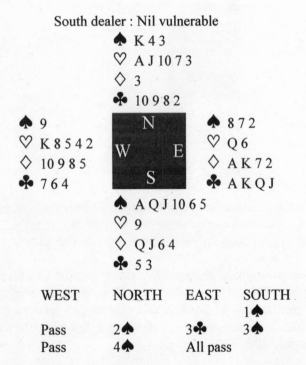

        ♠ K 4 3
        ♡ A J 10 7 3
        ◇ 3
        ♣ 10 9 8 2

♠ 9   ♠ 8 7 2
♡ K 8 5 4 2   ♡ Q 6
◇ 10 9 8 5   ◇ A K 7 2
♣ 7 6 4   ♣ A K Q J

        ♠ A Q J 10 6 5
        ♡ 9
        ◇ Q J 6 4
        ♣ 5 3

WEST	NORTH	EAST	SOUTH
			1♠
Pass	2♠	3♣	3♠
Pass	4♠	All pass	

East had no attractive action over 2♠ and opted for a 3♣ overcall. South competed with 3♠, but North treated it as a game invitation and bid game.

West began with the ♣4. East won with the ♣J and continued with the ♣Q. When the ♣K came at trick 3, declarer thought that the Old Master's ♣4-then-♣6 was an attempt at deception and so he ruffed with the ♠Q. A heart to the ace was followed by the ♢3. East won and played the ♣A. This time declarer did have to ruff high. The ♠J won and West discarded a heart.

After a diamond ruff, heart ruff, diamond ruff, this was the position:

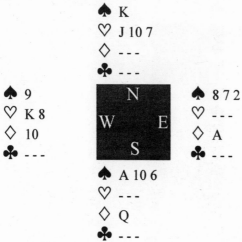

Needing the rest of the tricks declarer played the ♡7 from dummy. East inserted the ♠7, an uppercut, and South over-ruffed with the ♠10. The ♢Q was ruffed with the ♠K and when the ♡10 was led, East's ♠8 was a second uppercut. South over-ruffed with the ♠A. He was left with the ♠6 and I took trick thirteen, ended the spade nine.

I must admit that declarer could have done better if he had trusted the Old Master's carding and ruffed the third club low, but who bids a 4-card suit at the three-level? Let me show you another deal, said the spade nine, and this time the Old Master would have failed but for my presence.

The safe guard

The second story of the ♠9

Dealer South : East-West vulnerable

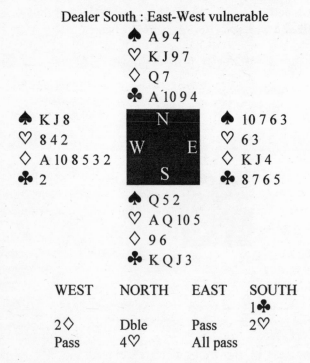

                    ♠ A 9 4
                    ♡ K J 9 7
                    ♢ Q 7
                    ♣ A 10 9 4

♠ K J 8   ♠ 10 7 6 3
♡ 8 4 2   N   ♡ 6 3
♢ A 10 8 5 3 2   W   E   ♢ K J 4
♣ 2   S   ♣ 8 7 6 5

                    ♠ Q 5 2
                    ♡ A Q 10 5
                    ♢ 9 6
                    ♣ K Q J 3

WEST	NORTH	EAST	SOUTH
			1♣
2♢	Dble	Pass	2♡
Pass	4♡	All pass	

I guess North's negative double was not perfect, the nine of
spades went on, but what would you suggest? I guess his plan was
to rebid 3♢ if South bid 2♠.

Anyway, West led the ♣2. The Old Master won and drew
trumps, followed by three rounds of clubs ending in hand.

He then played the ♢6. Fearful that the Old Master might have
started with ♢K-6, West rose with the ♢A and exited with a
diamond to East's king. This was now the position:

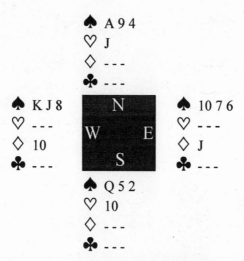

You can see how vital I was for the Old Master, said the spade nine. I was the guard for the spade suit. Without me the defence could take two spade tricks to beat the contract.

East switched to the ♣6: two – jack . . . The Old Master paused for barely a millisecond and played low in dummy. He figured that West would have the ♠K to justify the 2◇ jump-overcall at unfavourable vulnerability. West returned the ♠8, but the Old Master played me from dummy and captured East's ♠10. That gave us ten tricks where most declarers failed despite their 28 high card points.

The club ten piped up, What if East had led my counterpart?

Yes, East could have led the ♠10, replied the spade nine, but it makes no difference. On the ♠10, the Old Master would play the ♠Q. West covers and the Old Master ducks. The diamond exit gives a ruff-and-discard, while if West tries the ♠8, the Old Master finesses me. There is no way out.

That is not quite so, interjected the king of diamonds. East missed an opportunity to put the defence on the right path.

What is that? asked the spade nine.

The diamond king asked, When North doubled 2♢, what would redouble mean? Why not play that the redouble promises a top honour in partner's suit, perhaps the ace or the king. If South reached 4♡ after the redouble, West starts with the ♢A and another diamond. East wins and switches to a low spade and now your presence does the Old Master no good at all. If he ducks West's ♠J, a club or a trump exit leaves declarer without resource.

If you want to see a really nice play, which features me, of course, (modesty was not one of the diamond king's strong qualities), have a look at this:

The switching hour

The story of the ♢K

Dealer South : Both vulnerable

```
              ♠ K 10 9 5 2
              ♡ 7 4
              ♢ 9 7 2
              ♣ J 5 2
♠ 8 7                        ♠ J 6
♡ K 5           N            ♡ Q J 10 9 6
♢ K 8 6 5    W     E         ♢ A Q 10
♣ K 10 9 4 3    S            ♣ 8 7 6
              ♠ A Q 4 3
              ♡ A 8 3 2
              ♢ J 4 3
              ♣ A Q
```

WEST	NORTH	EAST	SOUTH
			1NT (1)
Pass	2♡ (2)	Pass	3♠ (3)
Pass	Pass	Pass	

(1) 15-17   (2) Transfer to spades   (3) 4 trumps and ruffing potential

The Old Master was playing with his wife, Jenny, said the diamond king. Not wanting to lead from any of the king-high suits, the Old Master started with the ♠7: ten – jack – ace. Declarer played the ♠3 to dummy's ♠10 and continued with the ♣2: eight – queen – king.

What do you think the Old Master should play next?

As East-West were playing reverse count, the ♣8 showed an odd number of clubs. The Old Master deduced that declarer would therefore have two or four clubs. If declarer had four clubs, there would be no possible discard for declarer on the clubs.

If declarer began with two clubs, then the hand pattern would be 4-3-4-2 or 4-4-3-2. If the former South has no useful discard on the ♣J. If declarer had 4-4 in the majors, then the ♣J could give declarer a diamond discard. South appeared to be marked with the A-Q in both black suits. If South had the ♡A, then South would have nothing useful in diamonds, while if South was 4-4-3-2 and had the ◇A, the defence could not prevent declarer from discarding a diamond on the ♣J. That meant the defence would collect only two hearts, a diamond and a club.

The diamond king pushed his chest out. Having reached this conclusion, the Old Master chose me as his lead at trick four. As you can see, the defenders now took three diamond tricks and a heart later to defeat 3♠.

I don't see what is so special about that, chirped the club jack. You can collect three diamond tricks even if the Old Master had switched to a low diamond.

You're missing the point, replied the diamond king. You remember how much the Old Master loved Jenny, how he doted on her, how they spent as much time together as possible. You remember how the Old Master looked after Jenny when she was dying of cancer. With her all the time. Never leaving her side.

The Old Master was exactly the same at the bridge table. As he looked after his life partner, he took care of his bridge partners, too. Suppose that the Old Master had shifted to a low diamond. Can you see what might have happened? East takes the ◇A and might easily switch to the ♡Q. Now declarer has nine tricks.

****

"Did you see that?" said the trainee nurse (just after the diamond king had spoken about the Old Master and Jenny). "I thought I saw a shudder run through his body."

"You must be mistaken," said the sister dismissively, "I didn't see anything."

****

I suppose it was a good play, the club jack conceded grudgingly to the diamond king, that the Old Master chose you at trick 4. Still, it is a lot harder when dummy has not yet appeared. Take a look at this auction:

WEST	NORTH	EAST	SOUTH
	1◇	Pass	1♠
Pass	4◇	Pass	4NT
Pass	6♣	Pass	6♡
Pass	7♠	All pass	

What do you think West should lead from:

♠ J 6
♡ 6 3
◇ J 10 9 5
♣ A J 10 6 3

Leading question

The story of the ♣J

Teams : Dealer North : East-West vulnerable

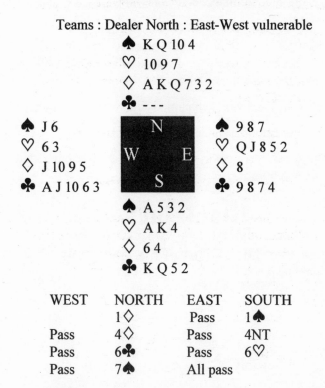

```
              ♠ K Q 10 4
              ♡ 10 9 7
              ◇ A K Q 7 3 2
              ♣ - - -
♠ J 6                        ♠ 9 8 7
♡ 6 3          N            ♡ Q J 8 5 2
◇ J 10 9 5   W   E          ◇ 8
♣ A J 10 6 3   S            ♣ 9 8 7 4
              ♠ A 5 3 2
              ♡ A K 4
              ◇ 6 4
              ♣ K Q 5 2
```

WEST	NORTH	EAST	SOUTH
	1◇	Pass	1♠
Pass	4◇	Pass	4NT
Pass	6♣	Pass	6♡
Pass	7♠	All pass	

4◇ showed a raise to 4♠ with long, strong diamonds. 6♣ showed two key cards plus a void in clubs, 6♡ asked for the ♠Q and 7♠ said, 'I have it.'

At both tables 7♠ was reached. One West led the ◇J, taken in dummy. After ♠K, spade to the ace and a spade to the queen, declarer set up the diamonds with one ruff and then led the ♣K, ♣A, ruffed. The diamonds were cashed and declarer made five spades including two ruffs, two hearts, five diamonds and the ♣Q.

At the other table the auction was the one given. As declarer was unaware of the bad break in diamonds, the Old Master chose me as his opening lead, boasted the club jack. Declarer ruffed in dummy, cashed ♠A and ♠K and then started on the diamonds. East ruffed the second diamond for one down and 17 Imps to the Old Master's team.

You think you're so smart, said the spade jack, but you were gone right at the start of the play. I was vital for the Old Master on this next deal and I stuck around right to the end.

But I was the key in a world championship, retorted the club jack.

Big deal, came back the spade jack. So was I.

These two jacks were always trying to best each other, but no one paid much attention.

Black jack

The stories of the ♠J

NORTH
♠ A J 3
♡ 10 5
♢ K 8 3
♣ A K 8 5 4

SOUTH
♠ K 8 7 4 2
♡ A 7 4
♢ A J 7
♣ Q 3

South is in 4♠, no opposition bidding, West began with the ♢10: three – two – jack. How should South continue?

This was the complete deal, said the spade jack.

Teams : Dealer South : North-South vulnerable

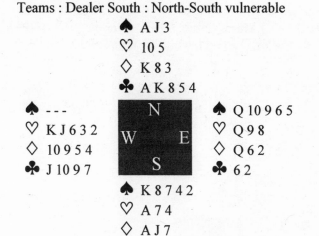

```
                    ♠ A J 3
                    ♡ 10 5
                    ◇ K 8 3
                    ♣ A K 8 5 4
    ♠ ---                          ♠ Q 10 9 6 5
    ♡ K J 6 3 2         N          ♡ Q 9 8
    ◇ 10 9 5 4      W       E      ◇ Q 6 2
    ♣ J 10 9 7          S          ♣ 6 2
                    ♠ K 8 7 4 2
                    ♡ A 7 4
                    ◇ A J 7
                    ♣ Q 3
```

WEST	NORTH	EAST	SOUTH
Kinston	*Zettner*	*Frawley*	*Old Master*
			1♠
Pass	2♣	Pass	2NT
Pass	4♠	All pass	

West led ◇10: three – two – jack. The Old Master considered his next move carefully. 'I am going to start the trumps next,' he thought, 'but should I begin with the ♠K or with a low trump to the jack? If the spades are 3-2, it will not matter, but what if they are 4-1?'

'The ♠K will save a trick if East began with the ♠Q singleton, but if East started with Q-10-6-5 or Q-9-6-5, playing the ♠K first will lose two tricks. So, the ♠K first has gains in one layout, while low to the jack gains in two.'

The Old Master played the ♠2 at trick 2. West discarded a heart and declarer took the ♠A. Next came a club to the queen, a low club back to the ♣A, followed by the ♣K. Frawley discarded the ◇Q while the Old Master threw a heart. Another club followed, East pitching his last diamond, while declarer ruffed.

Next came the ♡A and the ♡7. West rose with the ♡J, which won, and played a diamond, ruffed by East. This was now the position, said the spade jack, and notice that I am still involved in the fray.

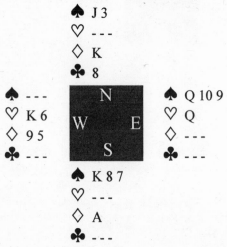

```
              ♠ J 3
              ♡ ---
              ◇ K
              ♣ 8
  ♠ ---         N          ♠ Q 10 9
  ♡ K 6                    ♡ Q
  ◇ 9 5      W     E       ◇ ---
  ♣ ---         S          ♣ ---
              ♠ K 8 7
              ♡ ---
              ◇ A
              ♣ ---
```

Declarer had lost two tricks and could afford only one more loser. East was on lead, but what could East do?

He exited with the ♡Q. The Old Master ruffed in hand and discarded the ♣8 from dummy. He now played the ◇A. East had to ruff and give declarer the last two tricks.

There I was right to the end and essential to the successful outcome. Mind you, said the spade jack, I was not always on the winning side. I remember this deal from a high stakes rubber bridge game where I thought we would beat declarer, but the Old Master prevailed again:

Dealer North : Nil vulnerable

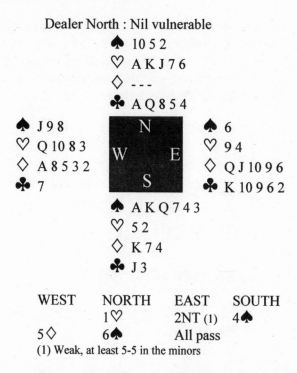

```
                        ♠ 10 5 2
                        ♡ A K J 7 6
                        ◇ - - -
                        ♣ A Q 8 5 4
        ♠ J 9 8                         ♠ 6
        ♡ Q 10 8 3          N           ♡ 9 4
        ◇ A 8 5 3 2     W       E       ◇ Q J 10 9 6
        ♣ 7                 S           ♣ K 10 9 6 2
                        ♠ A K Q 7 4 3
                        ♡ 5 2
                        ◇ K 7 4
                        ♣ J 3
```

WEST	NORTH	EAST	SOUTH
	1♡	2NT (1)	4♠
5◇	6♠	All pass	

(1) Weak, at least 5-5 in the minors

West started with the ♣7 and naturally the Old Master rose with dummy's ♣A. He continued with the ♡A, crossed to the ♠A and then finessed the ♡J. If my partner had two spades and one heart the slam would now be down, but the Old Master banked on the more common divisions in the major suits.

When the ♡J held, the Old Master cashed the ♡K and discarded the ♣J. He continued with the fourth heart, which he ruffed. This removed West's last heart and made dummy's fifth heart a winner. After a diamond ruff in dummy the Old Master played a club.

I thought to myself, 'Now we have him,' said the spade jack. 'West can over-ruff and play me and that will be cut declarer off from dummy.'

It did not work that way at all. The Old Master ruffed with the
♠K, ruffed a second diamond in dummy and then played
dummy's heart winner. On this he discarded the ◇K. My West
could ruff this, but I was left forlorn. Declarer ruffed the diamond
return, captured me with the ♠Q and had twelve tricks.

My heart bleeds for you, said the spade eight. At least there was
nothing your West player could do. Players tend to take me for
granted. Instead of appreciating the value I bring them they think
nothing of wasting my strength. Look what happened to me here:

Wasteland

The story of the ♠8

Dealer South : Nil vulnerable

```
              ♠ Q 9 7 5 4 3
              ♡ K 10 9
              ◇ Q
              ♣ K Q 9
♠ 10              N              ♠ A K J 6
♡ 8 6 4 2     W       E         ♡ 5 3
◇ J 9 5                         ◇ K 10 6 3 2
♣ 10 8 7 3 2      S             ♣ J 5
              ♠ 8 2
              ♡ A Q J 7
              ◇ A 8 7 4
              ♣ A 6 4
```

South opened 1NT, 15-17, East-West were silent and North bid
2♡, a transfer to spades. When South duly bid 2♠, North
decided to jump to 4♠. Not a great idea, but that's how it went.

West led the ♣3: nine – jack – ace. You won't believe what my declarer did next.

You don't mean . . .? said the spade jack.

Yes, my asinine South played me next, said the spade eight. What was the point of that? I was covered by the ♠10 and the ♠Q lost to the king. East eventually made four trump tricks for one down.

All my South had to do was play the ♠2 at trick 2 and cover the ♠10. The right time to play me was on the second round of trumps, letting East win with the ♠9. Next time the ♠J can knock out East's top spade and my brother, the ♠7, will do for the ♠6.

So simple, how could anyone get it wrong? Duh!

I know exactly how you feel, said the heart eight. The same thing keeps happening to me. Take a look at this:

NORTH
♠ Q 6 2
♡ K 8 2
◇ K Q J 7 5
♣ 10 5

SOUTH
♠ A K 7
♡ J 9 7 4
◇ A 9 8
♣ K Q 8

South has reached 4♡ and West leads the ♠J. South wins and continues with the ♡4: three – king – five. What do you think South should do next?

Heartbreaker

The story of the ♡8

Dealer East : Nil vulnerable

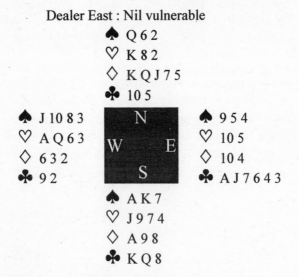

```
                    ♠ Q 6 2
                    ♡ K 8 2
                    ◇ K Q J 7 5
                    ♣ 10 5
♠ J 10 8 3                              ♠ 9 5 4
♡ A Q 6 3          N                    ♡ 10 5
◇ 6 3 2         W     E                 ◇ 10 4
♣ 9 2              S                    ♣ A J 7 6 4 3
                    ♠ A K 7
                    ♡ J 9 7 4
                    ◇ A 9 8
                    ♣ K Q 8
```

My side was playing Acol with a weak 1NT, said the heart eight. After East passed, South opened 1♡. North had stuck the ◇5 in between me and the ♡2. I wriggled around, trying to get his attention, but he took no notice and gave a limit raise to 3♡. South went on to 4♡ and West led the ♠J. When dummy went down, South saw the ◇5 in the wrong place and moved it to the end of the other diamonds.

Declarer had to lose a club and so he needed to restrict the trump losers to two. At trick 2 he played the ♡4: three – king – five. His next play was beyond comprehension.

You mean he . . . , said the spade eight.

Yes, interrupted the heart eight. That's exactly what I mean. He played me next. What was the need for that?

East played the ♡10 and the ♡J was taken by the queen. West now switched to the ♣9. As West had not led that at trick 1, East took the ♣9 to be top from a doubleton and so played the ♣3, an encouraging signal.

South won and tried the ♡7, but West went in with the ♡A and played a club to East's ace. East returned a club, ruffed by West for one down.

Incredible, said the spade eight. These players are such squanderers.

After the ♡K won, all South had to do, the heart eight went on, was to play the ♡2: ten – jack – queen. If West cashes the ♡A at trick 4, declarer can soon draw West's last trump. If instead of the ♡A West shifts to a club, ducked by East, South can cross to dummy with a spade or a diamond and lead a club or simply play a club out of hand.

As long as I am in dummy, said the heart eight, I protect declarer from the club ruff.

****

"His pulse rate is dropping," said the trainee nurse.

"Looks like the end is coming," said the sister.

****

Hey, you guys, said the club ace, what do you think you are doing? Those stories are just depressing. That's not what we want. The Old Master is already totally immersed in depression. We don't need any more. Don't you have a deal somewhere which is uplifting?

Terribly sorry, said the spade eight. You are quite right. How about this one?

Hard eight

The second story of the ♠8

Dealer South : Both vulnerable

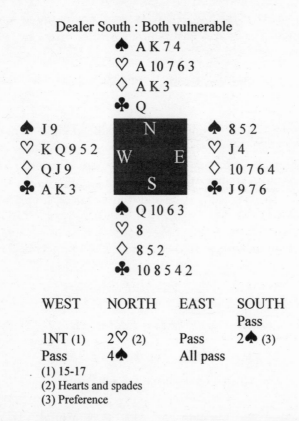

```
                    ♠ A K 7 4
                    ♡ A 10 7 6 3
                    ◇ A K 3
                    ♣ Q
  ♠ J 9               N              ♠ 8 5 2
  ♡ K Q 9 5 2    W         E         ♡ J 4
  ◇ Q J 9                             ◇ 10 7 6 4
  ♣ A K 3            S               ♣ J 9 7 6
                    ♠ Q 10 6 3
                    ♡ 8
                    ◇ 8 5 2
                    ♣ 10 8 5 4 2
```

WEST	NORTH	EAST	SOUTH
			Pass
1NT (1)	2♡ (2)	Pass	2♠ (3)
Pass	4♠	All pass	

(1) 15-17
(2) Hearts and spades
(3) Preference

With great strength in North's hearts, the Old Master led the ♠9:
four – two – ten. Declarer played a heart to the ace, heart ruff,
diamond to the ace, heart ruff. On this my East discarded a club.

Another diamond went to the king and a fourth heart was played,
ruffed this time with the ♠Q. East again pitched a club. This was
now the position:

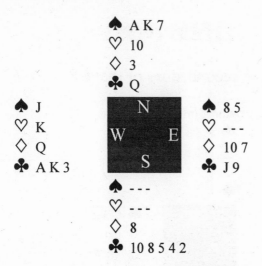

```
              ♠ A K 7
              ♡ 10
              ◇ 3
              ♣ Q
  ♠ J                        ♠ 8 5
  ♡ K                        ♡ - - -
  ◇ Q                        ◇ 10 7
  ♣ A K 3                    ♣ J 9
              ♠ - - -
              ♡ - - -
              ◇ 8
              ♣ 10 8 5 4 2
```

When South played a club, the Old Master took the ♣K, cashed the ◇Q and the ♡K. On the ♡K East threw the ♣J, his last club. When the Old Master played a club next, East was bound to score the ♠8 and so I put paid to the contract.

I have a good one, too, said the heart eight. May I have another turn, please?

Of course. Go ahead, said the club ace.

Heartfelt

The second story of the ♡8

Teams : Dealer North : Both vulnerable

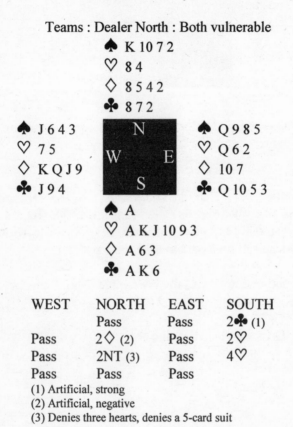

♠ K 10 7 2
♡ 8 4
◇ 8 5 4 2
♣ 8 7 2

♠ J 6 4 3
♡ 7 5
◇ K Q J 9
♣ J 9 4

♠ Q 9 8 5
♡ Q 6 2
◇ 10 7
♣ Q 10 5 3

♠ A
♡ A K J 10 9 3
◇ A 6 3
♣ A K 6

WEST	NORTH	EAST	SOUTH
	Pass	Pass	2♣ (1)
Pass	2◇ (2)	Pass	2♡
Pass	2NT (3)	Pass	4♡
Pass	Pass	Pass	

(1) Artificial, strong
(2) Artificial, negative
(3) Denies three hearts, denies a 5-card suit

If it wasn't for me, said the heart eight, the Old Master would almost certainly have failed. If you and I swapped places, he said to the heart six, declarer figures to lose a heart, two diamonds and a club.

Why doesn't South lose those tricks anyway? asked the heart six.

Because the Old Master was playing it, dummy.

Well, you needn't get nasty, said the heart six and walked off in a huff.

Don't you want to hear what happened?

Not interested.

The lead was the ♢K, shouted the heart eight after him. The Old Master took it, cashed the ♠A and played the ♡J next. What was East to do? If he did not take the ♡Q, he would lose, so he took it and returned the ♢10.

West overtook, cashed another diamond and played a fourth diamond. East discarded one card in each black suit, but it made no difference. The Old Master ruffed the fourth diamond, played the ♡3 to the ♡8 and discarded the ♣6 on the ♠K. After a spade ruff, the missing trump was drawn and the Old Master had ten tricks.

You know, I had almost the very same experience, said the spade seven. Do you think we might be related?

Access success

The story of the ♠7

Teams : Dealer North : East-West vulnerable

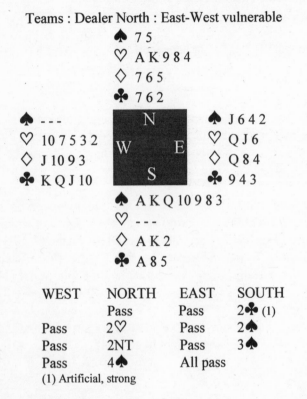

```
              ♠ 7 5
              ♡ A K 9 8 4
              ◇ 7 6 5
              ♣ 7 6 2
♠ - - -                        ♠ J 6 4 2
♡ 10 7 5 3 2      N            ♡ Q J 6
◇ J 10 9 3     W     E         ◇ Q 8 4
♣ K Q J 10        S            ♣ 9 4 3
              ♠ A K Q 10 9 8 3
              ♡ - - -
              ◇ A K 2
              ♣ A 8 5
```

WEST	NORTH	EAST	SOUTH
	Pass	Pass	2♣ (1)
Pass	2♡	Pass	2♠
Pass	2NT	Pass	3♠
Pass	4♠	All pass	

(1) Artificial, strong

West led the ♣K and the Old Master won with the ace.

This time I see it, interjected the heart six. I suppose the Old Master played the ♠10 next.

Precisely so, said the spade seven. If East declined the ♠J, he would never make it. When he took it and returned a club, West took two clubs and then shifted to the ◇J, but it was all over.

The Old Master won, played the ♠3 to me in dummy and discarded the diamond loser on the ♡A. The rest was routine.

We seem to have heard a lot from the spade suit, said the club ace, and very little from the minor suits.

I can give you a story, said the diamond three.

Low trick

The story of the ◇3

Pairs : Dealer North : North-South vulnerable

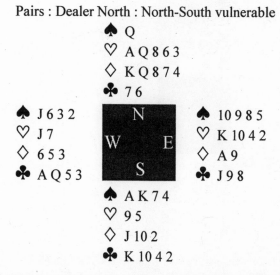

♠ Q
♡ A Q 8 6 3
◇ K Q 8 7 4
♣ 7 6

♠ J 6 3 2   ♠ 10 9 8 5
♡ J 7   ♡ K 10 4 2
◇ 6 5 3   ◇ A 9
♣ A Q 5 3   ♣ J 9 8

♠ A K 7 4
♡ 9 5
◇ J 10 2
♣ K 10 4 2

East-West were quiet. North opened 1♡, South responded 1♠ and over North's 2◇, South rebid 2NT. North raised to 3NT.

With no standout lead, the Old Master judged that East would have at least four hearts and so he began with the ♡J. Dummy's ♡Q lost to the king with East and, expecting the ♡J lead to be from J-10-x, South unblocked the ♡9 in order to finesse the ♡8 later. East switched to the ♠5, won in dummy.

It would be natural for declarer to start on the diamonds, but declarer decided to play a crafty ♣6: eight – ten – queen. This persuaded the Old Master that South must have length and strength in clubs and so he shifted to the ♢6, a high card to deny interest in the suit. Dummy's ♢K was taken by the ace and South unblocked the ♢10 to retain flexibility in the suit.

To attack declarer's entries, East returned the ♢9: jack – five – four. South cashed the ♠A and ♠K and, hoping for a few overtricks, finessed the ♡8 next, losing to the ♡10. This was now the position:

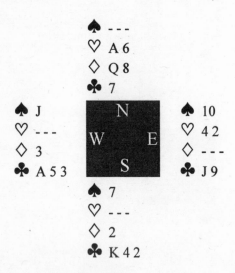

East returned the ♣J, king, ace, and back came the ♣3 to East's ♣9. East returned a spade to West's jack and dummy was now down to ♡A and ♢Q.

The Old Master was of course aware of the club spot cards that had been played and so he cashed the ♣5. Declarer now had to choose what to throw from dummy. Maybe South should have figured it out, but West's ♢6-then-♢5 suggested a doubleton. In that case West would have a heart left.

Accordingly, declarer threw the ♢Q from dummy. The Old
Master now played me, the ♢3, to win the last trick and I
captured declarer's ♢2 in the process.

Can you recall a deal where a three won the third round of a suit
and simultaneously captured a two? It made me as proud as punch
that I had become as powerful as an ace.

We aces might be powerful, said the heart ace, but it is vital that
we are played at the right moment. If a player slips up and does
not make best use of an ace, the cost can be extremely high.
Consider this problem:

Teams: West dealer : North-South vulnerable

```
              ♠ A 4
              ♡ 10 5 3
              ♢ A K 6
              ♣ K 9 8 7 4
```

```
                              ♠ 10 9 7 5 2
                              ♡ A 9 4
                              ♢ J 9 5 3
                              ♣ 2
```

WEST	NORTH	EAST	SOUTH
Pass	1♣	1♠ (1)	2♡
3♡ (2)	4♡	4♠	5♡
Pass	Pass	Pass	

(1) Flirting with the vulnerability   (2) Strong spade raise

West starts off with the ♠Q. Declarer wins with the ace, and
plays the ♡3 next.

Do you play the ♡A or do you play low?

Second-hand rose

The story of the ♥A

Teams : Dealer West : North-South vulnerable

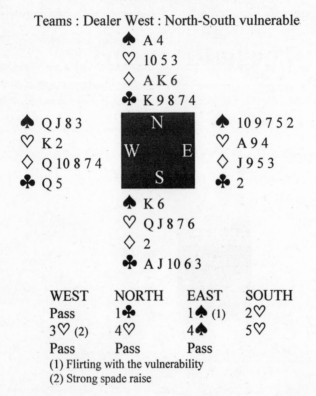

                    ♠ A 4
                    ♡ 10 5 3
                    ◇ A K 6
                    ♣ K 9 8 7 4

♠ Q J 8 3   ♠ 10 9 7 5 2
♡ K 2   ♡ A 9 4
◇ Q 10 8 7 4   ◇ J 9 5 3
♣ Q 5   ♣ 2

                    ♠ K 6
                    ♡ Q J 8 7 6
                    ◇ 2
                    ♣ A J 10 6 3

WEST	NORTH	EAST	SOUTH
Pass	1♣	1♠ (1)	2♡
3♡ (2)	4♡	4♠	5♡
Pass	Pass	Pass	

(1) Flirting with the vulnerability
(2) Strong spade raise

The Old Master liked to live in the fast lane when the vulnerability was favourable. Here his 1♠ overcall, which would not be condoned by the textbooks, led to a 4♠ sacrifice, which had the effect of pushing North-South too high. South took the push because of the potential good fit with North's club suit.

West led the ♠Q, taken by the ace in dummy. Declarer called for the ♡3 and the Old Master played the ♡A without hesitation.

He switched to the ♣2: jack – queen – king. West won the next heart and returned a club. East ruffed and that was one down.

You can see how important it was to play me at once, said the heart ace. If East plays a mechanical second-hand-low, the defence cannot obtain the club ruff and 5♡ will make. A similar problem occurred on this deal:

The bullet surprise

The second story of the ♡A

Teams : Dealer North : Both vulnerable

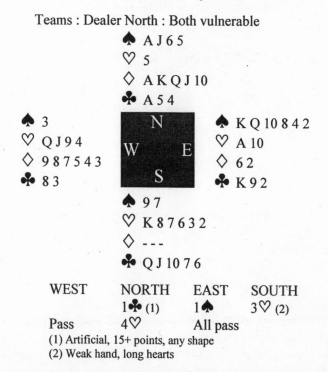

```
              ♠ A J 6 5
              ♡ 5
              ◇ A K Q J 10
              ♣ A 5 4
  ♠ 3                        ♠ K Q 10 8 4 2
  ♡ Q J 9 4      N           ♡ A 10
  ◇ 9 8 7 5 4 3  W   E       ◇ 6 2
  ♣ 8 3             S        ♣ K 9 2
              ♠ 9 7
              ♡ K 8 7 6 3 2
              ◇ - - -
              ♣ Q J 10 7 6
```

WEST	NORTH	EAST	SOUTH
	1♣ (1)	1♠	3♡ (2)
Pass	4♡	All pass	

(1) Artificial, 15+ points, any shape
(2) Weak hand, long hearts

West began with the ♠3, taken by the ace. South discarded the spade loser on the ◇A and played the ♡5 next. What would you have done as East?

The diamond seven piped up, Makes no difference, does it? Declarer always has three trump losers and a club to lose.

Not necessarily, said the heart ace.

Suppose East plays low. South wins with the ♡K and plays a second trump. East wins with the ♡A and plays a top spade. South ruffs and West over-ruffs. Now West switches to a club. Declarer might place East with the ♣K for the vulnerable overcall and reject the club finesse. If South takes the ♣A and rattles off the diamonds, all of South's clubs vanish and the contract makes.

Is that what happened? the diamond seven asked.

Not with the Old Master sitting East. He rose with the me on the first round of trumps, said the heart ace, and played a top spade. South ruffed low and West over-ruffed. He switched to the ♣8 and now declarer did not have the option of playing the ♣A to run the diamonds. East had a trump left and could ruff in on the third diamond.

You are lucky, said the diamond seven. Declarer usually has a choice whether to play you or not. We lower cards are often just caught up in the wash.

You must have some triumphs, too, said the heart ace.

Yes, but usually in quite a different situation from the ones you have shown us.

Why don't you tell us about them?

Get shorty

The stories of the ◇7

I was the favourite of the Old Master on a few deals from the semi-finals of a world championship, said the diamond seven.

Teams : Dealer North : North-South vulnerable

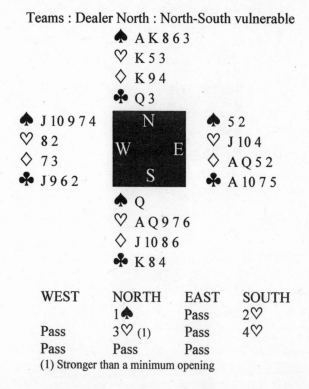

```
              ♠ A K 8 6 3
              ♡ K 5 3
              ◇ K 9 4
              ♣ Q 3
♠ J 10 9 7 4      N        ♠ 5 2
♡ 8 2                      ♡ J 10 4
◇ 7 3         W       E    ◇ A Q 5 2
♣ J 9 6 2         S        ♣ A 10 7 5
              ♠ Q
              ♡ A Q 9 7 6
              ◇ J 10 8 6
              ♣ K 8 4
```

WEST	NORTH	EAST	SOUTH
	1♠	Pass	2♡
Pass	3♡ (1)	Pass	4♡
Pass	Pass	Pass	

(1) Stronger than a minimum opening

The Old Master chose me as his opening lead, said the diamond seven. Declarer played low from dummy and the defence took the ◇Q, ◇A, ◇2 ruffed and the ♣A. There was no point starting with a spade, as dummy had bid that suit, and with such a weak hand, a short suit lead looked a good chance.

The same thing happened at the other table, so there was no swing. In the other semi-final, West led a club against 4♡ and declarer had no problems. At their other table North was declarer in 4♡ after opening 1NT and a transfer sequence by South. Played by North, 4♡ is unbeatable. Again no swing.

This happened later in the same match, said the diamond seven:

Dealer North : North-South vulnerable

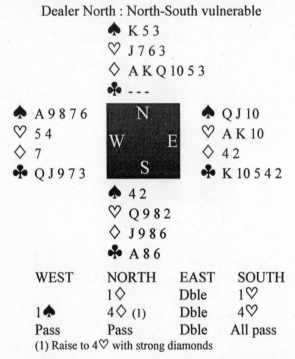

```
              ♠ K 5 3
              ♡ J 7 6 3
              ◇ A K Q 10 5 3
              ♣ - - -
♠ A 9 8 7 6        N        ♠ Q J 10
♡ 5 4                       ♡ A K 10
◇ 7           W       E     ◇ 4 2
♣ Q J 9 7 3        S        ♣ K 10 5 4 2
              ♠ 4 2
              ♡ Q 9 8 2
              ◇ J 9 8 6
              ♣ A 8 6
```

WEST	NORTH	EAST	SOUTH
	1◇	Dble	1♡
1♠	4◇ (1)	Dble	4♡
Pass	Pass	Dble	All pass

(1) Raise to 4♡ with strong diamonds

The Old Master chose me again and dummy won with the ◇A. On a low heart East took the ♡K and returned a diamond ruffed. The Old Master cashed the ♠A and the ♡A later meant one down. On any lead but the ◇7 or the ♠A and switch to the ◇7, 4♡ cannot be defeated.

Don't go selling us short, said the club seven. We sevens have useful roles other than just as opening leads. See how the Old Master put me to good use on this deal:

Chip off the old unblock

The story of the ♣7

Pairs : Dealer South : East-West vulnerable

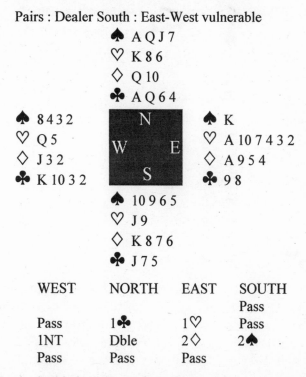

```
                    ♠ A Q J 7
                    ♡ K 8 6
                    ◇ Q 10
                    ♣ A Q 6 4
   ♠ 8 4 3 2            N            ♠ K
   ♡ Q 5         W           E      ♡ A 10 7 4 3 2
   ◇ J 3 2                           ◇ A 9 5 4
   ♣ K 10 3 2         S             ♣ 9 8
                    ♠ 10 9 6 5
                    ♡ J 9
                    ◇ K 8 7 6
                    ♣ J 7 5
```

WEST	NORTH	EAST	SOUTH
			Pass
Pass	1♣	1♡	Pass
1NT	Dble	2◇	2♠
Pass	Pass	Pass	

North doubled 1NT to show extra values and when the Old Master bid 2♠, North-South had found their 4-4 fit.

West led the ♡Q: king – ace – nine, and East returned the ♡7, taken by the ♡J. The Old Master ran the ♠10, losing to the bare king. When East played the ♡10, the Old Master ruffed with his ♠9 and West discarded the ◇2.

A diamond to dummy's queen lost to the ◇A and East played the ◇4 back. The Old Master played his ◇K, West following with the ◇J. East discarded a heart on the ♠5 to the ♠A.

The Old Master pieced together West's shape. Four spades, two
hearts and three diamonds meant that West also had four clubs.
With only the ♡Q and ◇J in high cards so far, West figured to
have the ♣K as well. The Old Master drew West's remaining trumps
and discarded the ◇10 from dummy. These cards remained:

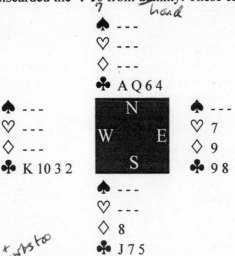

The Old Master played the ♣Q from dummy, and discarded me
from his hand, went on the club seven. West won with the ♣K
and returned the ♣2: four – nine – jack. Knowing West had only
clubs left, the Old Master finished off the play with the ♣5: three
– six . . . the ♣A was declarer's ninth trick and +140 meant a fine
match-point score.

Sometimes the best function is simply to get out of the way, said
the club seven. That's what the Old Master did with me. You can
see what would have happened if he had played the ♣5 under the
♣Q. West wins and returns a low club to the nine and jack. Now
when the ♣7 is played, West plays low and declarer can make
only eight tricks. At Imps that overtrick would not amount to
much, but at pairs it is the difference between average-minus and
a good score.

****

The doctors were just about to leave the Old Master's ward.

"There is good news and bad news," said the surgeon. "The pulse rate is back to normal, but his condition has not improved beyond that."

"The coma is as deep as ever," said the Australian coma expert. "There was no reaction to physical stimulation."

****

That's not all bad news, commented the spade ace. It suggests that there has been reaction to mental stimulation. We must keep up the good work. Who wants to go next?

We've heard very little from our wee ones, said the club king. Perhaps some of them have a tale to tell.

Oh, yes, said the heart two.

After listening to the stories from the others, the heart two's tears had dried.

I was very helpful to the Old Master on this deal, the heart two went on. In fact I was able to solve his problem.

How could a mere two solve a problem? murmured the spade ten.

Let's hear what he has to say, replied the club ten.

Voyage of discovery

The story of the ♡2

Teams : Dealer North : Both vulnerable

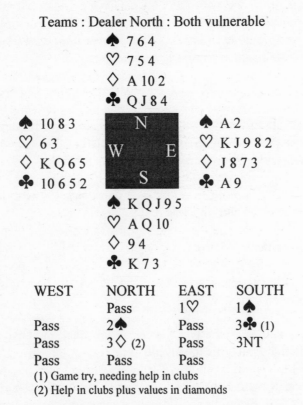

♠ 7 6 4
♡ 7 5 4
♦ A 10 2
♣ Q J 8 4

♠ 10 8 3
♡ 6 3
♦ K Q 6 5
♣ 10 6 5 2

♠ A 2
♡ K J 9 8 2
♦ J 8 7 3
♣ A 9

♠ K Q J 9 5
♡ A Q 10
♦ 9 4
♣ K 7 3

WEST	NORTH	EAST	SOUTH
	Pass	1♡	1♠
Pass	2♠	Pass	3♣ (1)
Pass	3♦ (2)	Pass	3NT
Pass	Pass	Pass	

(1) Game try, needing help in clubs
(2) Help in clubs plus values in diamonds

West led the ♡6, four from dummy and the Old Master paused
for just a second. Then my big moment came, said the heart two.
The Old Master played me at trick one!

Why would the Old Master do that? asked the spade ten. Why
not the ♡K?

Because he was not sure of West's heart holding from the ♡6 lead, replied the heart two. It could be from Q-10-6 or from 6-3. He used me to discover which it was.

South took trick one with the ♡10 and played the ♣3: two – queen – ace. South's plan was to create an entry in dummy to make the first spade lead from dummy. That would cater for East having the ♠A bare.

Knowing from South's ♡10 at trick one that South had started with A-Q-10, the Old Master won with the ♣A and switched to the ◇3. The defence could now collect three diamonds and two aces to take 3NT one down. If East plays a second heart after taking a black ace, declarer will succeed.

Yes, very nice, very nice, indeed, growled the heart nine, but I have to say I don't like the way Old Master always favours the little ones. He could use us, the more mature ones, from time to time. On your deal it would have been all right if the Old Master had played me. That would have provided the same information. I'm sure that the heart eight will agree with me.

The heart eight nodded.

We both felt slighted, the heart nine went on. Of course, the Old Master had to choose one of us, but invariably in these situations he gives you youngsters priority. It just isn't fair. You solved the Old Master's problem on that deal, but I helped him just as much on this deal. The difference is that I was not in the Old Master's hand. I was with his partner, Walter Zettner.

Walter wall defence

The story of the ♡9

Teams : Dealer South : East-West vulnerable

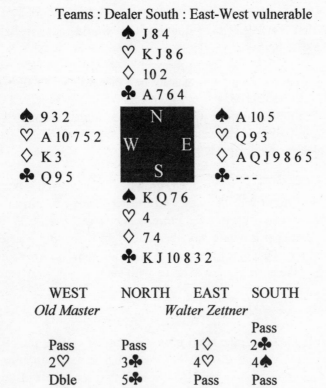

```
                    ♠ J 8 4
                    ♡ K J 8 6
                    ◊ 10 2
                    ♣ A 7 6 4
♠ 9 3 2                              ♠ A 10 5
♡ A 10 7 5 2          N              ♡ Q 9 3
◊ K 3          W           E         ◊ A Q J 9 8 6 5
♣ Q 9 5              S               ♣ - - -
                    ♠ K Q 7 6
                    ♡ 4
                    ◊ 7 4
                    ♣ K J 10 8 3 2
```

WEST	NORTH	EAST	SOUTH
Old Master		*Walter Zettner*	
			Pass
Pass	Pass	1◊	2♣
2♡	3♣	4♡	4♠
Dble	5♣	Pass	Pass
Dble	Pass	Pass	Pass

It seems that South will be two down in 5♣ doubled, since he is sure to take the winning position in clubs. That result will be fine in itself since 4♡ was almost certain to fail, perhaps doubled. When Walter picked the layout of the hand he was able to use me to help partner take declarer three down.

The Old Master began with the ◇K and Walter overtook with the ◇A in case the ◇K was singleton. When he cashed the ◇Q and all followed, he formed a mental picture of the unseen hands. South was known to have exactly two diamonds and at most one heart, since West's 2♡ response indicated five hearts at least.

Therefore South had ten black cards. South figured to have good spades to suggest 4♠ as a contract, so South's pattern should be 4-1-2-6. With 5-5 in the black suits, South would have chosen a 1♠ overcall, not 2♣. Give South decent spades and West should have the ♡A for the two-level response.

Walter knew that if he played a third diamond, South would simply discard the heart loser. He therefore switched to hearts to ensure scoring a trick there. He specially chose me, the heart nine, to tell partner not to return a heart. When we switch to a new suit in the middle game it is high-hate, low-like.

The Old Master recognized the significance of partner's play and shifted to the ♠9, high-hate. Walter took the ♠A and now played a third diamond. This created a trump trick for West no matter how declarer played and the result was +500.

If declarer discarded a spade or ruffed low, West's ♣9 would force out the ♣A. If South ruffed with the ♣J or ♣10, the more likely play, the Old Master would discard and make a trump trick by force.

I enjoyed that deal, too, said the club nine. I was a vital element. If I had been in declarer's hand, it would not be possible to take 5♣ more than two down. Walter did do well to envisage me in the Old Master's hand.

You probably know that the club seven and I are good friends. Whenever we go together we seem to do well. This happened not too long ago.

Pin Friends

The stories of the ♣9

Teams : Dealer East : North-South vulnerable

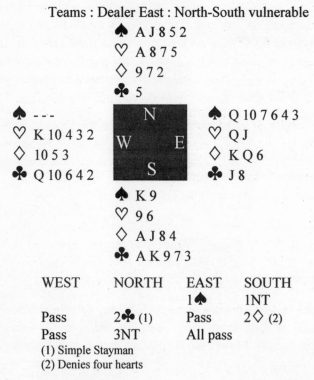

```
                    ♠ A J 8 5 2
                    ♡ A 8 7 5
                    ◇ 9 7 2
                    ♣ 5
♠ - - -                              ♠ Q 10 7 6 4 3
♡ K 10 4 3 2          N              ♡ Q J
◇ 10 5 3         W         E         ◇ K Q 6
♣ Q 10 6 4 2          S              ♣ J 8
                    ♠ K 9
                    ♡ 9 6
                    ◇ A J 8 4
                    ♣ A K 9 7 3
```

WEST	NORTH	EAST	SOUTH
		1♠	1NT
Pass	2♣ (1)	Pass	2◇ (2)
Pass	3NT	All pass	

(1) Simple Stayman
(2) Denies four hearts

West led the ♣4: five – jack – ace and the Old Master cashed the ♠K next. Perhaps West might provide a useful singleton. When West discarded a heart, the spade position was revealed. Not very helpful.

How to continue? With only six top tricks, 3NT looked a long way off. That's when the Old Master had the bright idea to play me next, said the club nine. It would force the defenders to make the running and perhaps they might be helpful.

Not only that, said the club nine, but I was also able to pin that nasty ♣8.

I beg your pardon, the club eight remonstrated.

Just kidding, just kidding, but when the ♣10 won and the ♣8 fell, West could not return a club without giving declarer an extra trick. By playing me the Old Master had promoted my mate, the club seven, into a useful threat.

As expected, West switched and, fearful of leading from the ♡K into the 1NT bidder, he exited with the ◇3: two – queen – four. East tried the ♡Q, which held, then the ♡J, taken by the ace.

The Old Master played the ◇7 and finessed the ◇J. When the ◇A collected the missing diamonds, these cards remained:

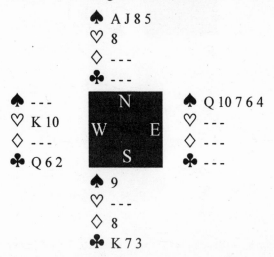

So far declarer had taken one spade, one heart, one club and two diamonds. He had three more winners, but needed four. No problem for the Old Master. He cashed the ◇8 and the ♣K, discarding dummy's two hearts. As East was known to be down to spades only, the ♠9 went to the ♠J. Whether East took it or discarded, the Old Master had the two tricks he needed to make his game.

Yes, that was good, said the club seven, but we have had other great times together and not only in declarer play. You remember that time we also combined to nullify the value of declarer's ♣6?

Indeed, I do, said the club nine. This was the deal:

Teams : Dealer South : North-South vulnerable

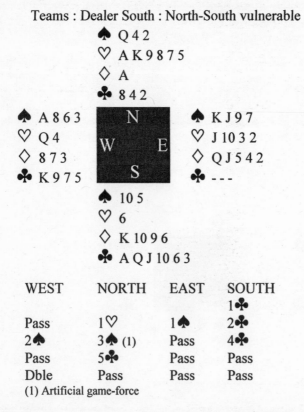

♠ Q 4 2
♡ A K 9 8 7 5
♢ A
♣ 8 4 2

♠ A 8 6 3   ♠ K J 9 7
♡ Q 4   ♡ J 10 3 2
♢ 8 7 3   ♢ Q J 5 4 2
♣ K 9 7 5   ♣ - - -

♠ 10 5
♡ 6
♢ K 10 9 6
♣ A Q J 10 6 3

WEST	NORTH	EAST	SOUTH
			1♣
Pass	1♡	1♠	2♣
2♠	3♠ (1)	Pass	4♣
Pass	5♣	Pass	Pass
Dble	Pass	Pass	Pass

(1) Artificial game-force

The contract was always one down, but we wanted more. We wanted to show that we were ruthless.

The Old Master opened with the ♠A and continued with the ♠3: four – jack – ten. East continued with the ♠K, ruffed. Declarer played a diamond to the ace, followed by the ♣2. When East discarded a diamond, declarer followed with the ♣Q.

The Old Master won with the ♣K and thought about his next move for a moment. Then he played me from his hand, said the club nine. You can see what would have happened if he had chosen the ♣5 instead. South would have won the trick with the ♣6, ruffed a diamond in dummy, cashed the ♡A, ♡K to discard the other losing diamond and then ruffed a heart with a high club. He could then draw trumps and make ten tricks.

But when I was played, said the club nine, it was like an uppercut, since I knocked out a high trump from declarer, and cleared a path for the club seven to prevail. Declarer captured me with the ♣10, ruffed the ◇9, cashed the ♡A and discarded the ◇10 on the ♡K, but this was now the position:

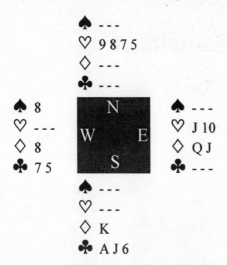

When the forced heart came from dummy, no matter whether he ruffed high or low, declarer could not avoid West's ♣7 scoring a trick for two down and −500.

You did make the best of your opportunity, given the circumstances, said the spade five.

What do you mean? asked the club nine.

It's common enough, said the spade five. Declarer makes an error and you must seize the moment, make sure you capitalize on it. Missed opportunities often do not show up on the score-sheet and players are not quick to point out their own lack of enterprise. On your deal after declarer ruffed the third spade, crossed to the ◇A and led a trump, he should have gone up with the ♣A when East showed out. Now diamond ruff, ♡A, ♡K, pitching the ◇10, and then a club to the ten restricts the defence to three tricks.

I wasn't being critical, the spade five said, Just making an observation. The same sort of thing happened to me and allowed the Old Master to make use of me to score an extra trick, too. This was the deal . . .

Knockout blow

The story of the ♠5

Teams : Dealer North : Nil vulnerable

```
                    ♠ J 6
                    ♡ 8 6
                    ◇ A K 8 6 4 2
                    ♣ A K 7
 ♠ K 8 7 4           N           ♠ 5 3
 ♡ A K 10 9 7 3   W     E        ♡ Q 5 4
 ◇ Q 3              S            ◇ J 10 9 5
 ♣ 6                             ♣ 10 5 3 2
                    ♠ A Q 10 9 2
                    ♡ J 2
                    ◇ 7
                    ♣ Q J 9 8 4
```

In a teams event with duplicated boards most of the field were playing in diamond part-scores North-South. In our match both tables reached 4♠. Against our team-mates West cashed the ♡A, ♡K and switched to the ♣6. Declarer won in dummy, finessed in spades and made ten tricks for +420. At our table it went this way:

WEST	NORTH	EAST	SOUTH
	1NT	Pass	2♡ (1)
Dble	Pass (2)	Pass	3♣
Pass	3♢	Pass	3♠
Pass	4♠	All pass	

(1) Transfer to spades   (2) Two spades exactly

Here, too, the Old Master began with the ♡A and ♡K and Zettner signalled a 3-card holding. With East holding the ♡Q, East could not have any useful high card for defence and so the Old Master persisted with a third heart, even though it gave declarer a ruff and discard.

Here's where our good luck stepped in. Declarer was not paying attention to the heart signals or perhaps did not believe them, because he ruffed with dummy's ♠J and not the ♠6. That was not the end of it. He was still all right if he had then played the ♠6 to the ♠A and continued with a top spade, but he erred by playing the ♠6: three – queen – king.

That's what I meant earlier, said the spade five, about seizing the moment. The Old Master did just that. After capturing the ♠Q, he played a fourth heart. He was hoping for the ♠9 with East, but I was just as good. I ruffed the heart and South over-ruffed with the ♠9. I had knocked out one of declarer's equally high trumps.

South could cash the ♠A and ♠10, but the Old Master's ♠8 became the setting trick.

Hmmph, snorted the heart seven. You think you are all so smart, but in my case I did not have to rely on any error by declarer. The Old Master laid out the defence like a blueprint and declarer had no escape.

Seven Up

The story of the ♡7

Rubber bridge : Dealer South : Nil vulnerable

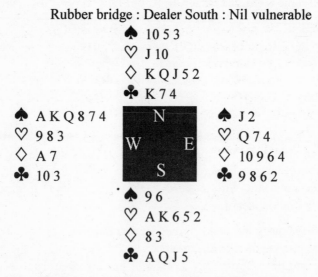

```
                ♠ 10 5 3
                ♡ J 10
                ◇ K Q J 5 2
                ♣ K 7 4
♠ A K Q 8 7 4         N          ♠ J 2
♡ 9 8 3          W        E      ♡ Q 7 4
◇ A 7                 S          ◇ 10 9 6 4
♣ 10 3                          ♣ 9 8 6 2
                ♠ 9 6
                ♡ A K 6 5 2
                ◇ 8 3
                ♣ A Q J 5
```

The family was having a rubber bridge game with father-daughter playing against mother-son:

WEST	NORTH	EAST	SOUTH
O.M.	Jenny	Kate	Harry
			1♡
3♠	4◇	Pass	4♡
Pass	Pass	Pass	

The Old Master began with the ♠K, then the ♠A. Next he cashed the ◇A. At trick 4 he switched back to spades, but he did not play the ♠Q, he played the ♠8.

Harry put on the ♠10 from dummy and Kate went into thought.

"Come on, come on,' said Harry, "Play."

"Let me think," Kate responded.

What she thinking about? It was what had happened so far. From the bidding father obviously had the ♠Q yet he had played the ♠8 with the ♠10 in dummy. Also, strangely, father had cashed the ◇A first and set up all of dummy's diamonds. He was trying to send her a message, but what was it?

As Harry clearly had no valúes in spades or in diamonds, he must have the A-K in hearts and the ♣A. In that case . . . then she saw it. Her ♥Q was doomed anyway. If she ruffed with the ♥Q it would do no good. Harry would over-ruff and the ♥J and ♥10 would become winners. She needed the ♥Q to take one of those heart honours out of contention. There was one faint hope and so she took me out . . . the heart seven stuck his seven pips out proudly . . . and played me on the ♠10.

Of course there was nothing Harry could do. He had to over-ruff. A club to the king was followed by the ♥J: queen – ace. A heart back to the ♥10 left the Old Master with the ♥9, the top trump and the setting trick.

"Well done, Kate," said the Old Master, "Very well done, indeed."

"Oh, I did it, I did it," shrieked Kate. She raced around the table, hugged her father and kissed his bald patch.

"Oh, come on," said Harry. "Whose deal is it?"

****

"Doctor, you'd better come quickly. It's room 13."

"What's happened?"

"A thick mucous has spread over the Old Master's eyes."

The doctor was there at once. He examined the Old Master.

"How strange," he said. "That's not mucous. Those are tears in his eyes. He must be reliving either some painful or some very tender memories. Or perhaps both."

****

Is that a good sign or a bad sign? asked the diamond queen.

The doctor did not suggest that this was anything bad, said the heart queen, and it means that his mind is active. It seems he has tuned in to what we are doing.

In that case I can understand why there are tears in his eyes after that last deal, said the spade king. He was about to elaborate, but thought better of it. After all, they all knew what had happened. Anyway, let's continue, he said, it's important we keep up this good work. Who wants to be next?

I have a little triumph, said the ◇5.

Go right ahead then.

How low can you go?

The story of the ◇5

Rubber bridge : Dealer South : Both vulnerable

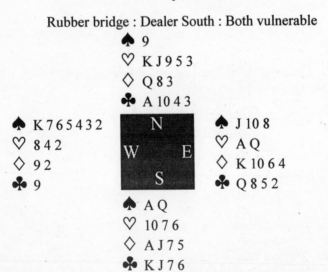

```
              ♠ 9
              ♡ K J 9 5 3
              ◇ Q 8 3
              ♣ A 10 4 3
♠ K 7 6 5 4 3 2    N        ♠ J 10 8
♡ 8 4 2                     ♡ A Q
◇ 9 2         W    E        ◇ K 10 6 4
♣ 9                S        ♣ Q 8 5 2
              ♠ A Q
              ♡ 10 7 6
              ◇ A J 7 5
              ♣ K J 7 6
```

South opened 1NT, 15-17, and North bid 2◇, transfer to hearts. After South bid 2♡, North rebid 3NT. South converted to 4♡.

Since he had three hearts and potential for ruffing in spades, the Old Master removed 3NT to 4♡. He received the ♣9 lead. 'That could be a doubleton,' he thought, 'but it is more likely to be a singleton.' He covered the ♣9 with the ten and captured the ♣Q.

Next came the ♡6: four – jack – queen. East returned the ♣2 and West ruffed declarer's ♣6. West switched to the ♢9: queen – king – ace and the next heart removed the missing trumps. East was in with the ♡A and shifted to the ♠J.

'That could be from K-J-10,' thought the Old Master. 'If I take the finesse and it works, I can ditch dummy's diamond loser on the ♠A. On the other hand if the ♠K is with West I am down.'

The Old Master made up his mind instantly. He took the ♠A, and continued with the ♠Q, covered by the ♠K and ruffed in dummy. This was now the position:

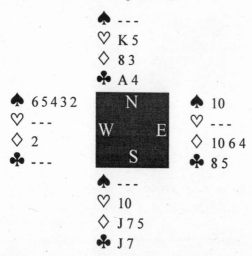

```
              ♠ - - -
              ♡ K 5
              ♢ 8 3
              ♣ A 4
  ♠ 65432      N        ♠ 10
  ♡ - - -   W     E     ♡ - - -
  ♢ 2          S        ♢ 10 6 4
  ♣ - - -               ♣ 8 5
              ♠ - - -
              ♡ 10
              ♢ J 7 5
              ♣ J 7
```

The Old Master led the ♢8 from dummy: ten – jack – two. He cashed the ♣J and crossed to the ♣A. Then came the ♢3: four and he finessed the five. I know there can be a lower finesse, said the diamond five, but I was proud to be part of one of the lowest ever. When I won the trick, the Old Master had made 4♡.

It's always good to be in the Old Master's hand, because he takes excellent care of you, said the club six. When you are in some other players' hands, you are often scorned, neglected, discarded. Here is an example . . .

Pitch black

The story of the ♣6

Rubber bridge : Dealer West : Both vulnerable

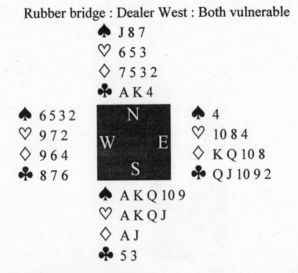

```
                    ♠ J 8 7
                    ♡ 6 5 3
                    ♢ 7 5 3 2
                    ♣ A K 4
     ♠ 6 5 3 2          N          ♠ 4
     ♡ 9 7 2                        ♡ 10 8 4
     ♢ 9 6 4        W       E       ♢ K Q 10 8
     ♣ 8 7 6           S            ♣ Q J 10 9 2
                    ♠ A K Q 10 9
                    ♡ A K Q J
                    ♢ A J
                    ♣ 5 3
```

South opened 2♣ in fourth seat and North responded 2NT to show a balanced positive. South rebid 3♠ and North cue-bid 4♣ to show spade support and the ♣A. After South cue-bid 4♢, North showed the ♣K with 5♣. That was enough to persuade South to jump to 7♠.

The lead was the ♠2 and declarer played off his five trumps. East followed once and then discarded the ♣Q, ♣2, followed by the ♢10 and ♢8 (high-low encouraging). Meanwhile on the fifth spade my West had to decide what to discard.

It looked pretty clear that East must have started with five clubs headed by the Q-J-10 and with East showing strength in diamonds declarer must have good hearts. A heart discard is safe and a diamond must be all right as well. That's what the Old Master would have chosen.

What does my West do? moaned the club six. He chooses me as his first discard. Look what happens next. Declarer plays off the top hearts and they break 3-3. This is now the position:

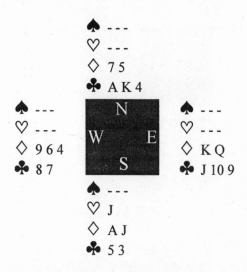

When the ♡J is played, it does not matter what West does, but in fact he lets go a diamond, as does dummy. Now East is squeezed. If he throws a diamond, the ♢A captures the remaining diamond honour and the ♢J is high, so he throws the ♣9. South plays off the ♢A, followed by the ♣A, ♣K and the ♣4 is declarer's thirteenth trick.

You were unlucky, said the club eight. West could just as easily have taken the club seven or me for the first discard, but I know exactly how you feel. Almost the same thing happened to me.

Throwaway line

The story of the ♣8

Imps : Dealer North : East-West vulnerable

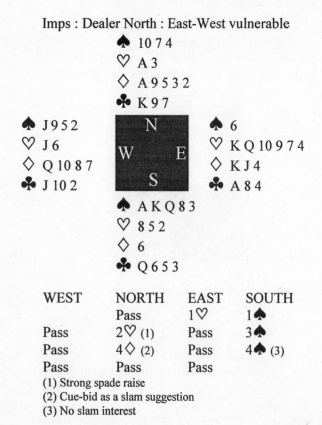

```
                    ♠ 10 7 4
                    ♥ A 3
                    ♦ A 9 5 3 2
                    ♣ K 9 7
     ♠ J 9 5 2                        ♠ 6
     ♥ J 6                            ♥ K Q 10 9 7 4
     ♦ Q 10 8 7                       ♦ K J 4
     ♣ J 10 2                         ♣ A 8 4
                    ♠ A K Q 8 3
                    ♥ 8 5 2
                    ♦ 6
                    ♣ Q 6 5 3
```

WEST	NORTH	EAST	SOUTH
	Pass	1♥	1♠
Pass	2♥ (1)	Pass	3♠
Pass	4♦ (2)	Pass	4♠ (3)
Pass	Pass	Pass	

(1) Strong spade raise
(2) Cue-bid as a slam suggestion
(3) No slam interest

West led ♣J: seven – four – queen. Declarer was theoretically in good shape after the lead since there are four spade tricks, the ♥A and a heart ruff, the ♦A and three club tricks. Of course, South did not know about the spade loser or that clubs were 3-3. South did not want to risk a club ruff before arranging the heart ruff and so, at trick 2, declarer played the ♥2: six – three – four.

Not keen to touch the clubs again West switched to the ◇7. South took the ◇A, cashed the ♡A, played a spade to the ace and led the third heart. On this West threw the ♣10. Declarer ruffed the heart in dummy and returned to hand with a spade to the king, while East discarded a heart. This was the ending:

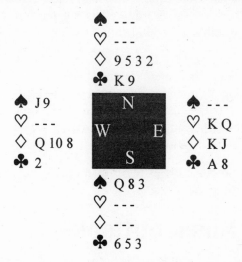

Declarer cashed the ♠Q, pitching a diamond from dummy. What do you think East threw? asked the club eight.

A heart, of course, said the ace of clubs. The hearts were obviously useless.

Indeed so, said the club eight. If the Old Master had been East, the discard would have been a heart. No, my East had to throw me away. He must have thought I was of no value, but I had become the key to the hand.

Once I was gone, declarer played the ♣3 to dummy's ♣9. East took the ace, but it did not matter what he did, declarer was now safe. Had East returned a diamond, South ruffs and plays a club. West cannot afford to ruff and so the ♣K wins and declarer now ruffs a diamond for the tenth trick.

In fact East played a heart back. South ruffed, West over-ruffed. Declarer jettisoned dummy's ♣K and claimed the rest.

If East had discarded the ♡Q instead, South was doomed. A club to the nine takes out East's ace, but the ♡K comes back. South ruffs and West over-ruffs, but South cannot afford to discard the ♣K this time, as South's clubs are not high yet. A diamond takes out South's last trump with the clubs still blocked. .

It is much easier for us, said the ace of clubs, since we know what has to be done, but mere humans are prone to make mistakes. Discarding is a tough area, so even though it looks automatic to us to do the right thing, and even though the Old Master also does the right thing almost all the time, we must make allowances for the human factor.

Opening leads is another tough area for humans, he went on. Take a look at this problem . . .

Black outlook

The stories of the ♣A

Imps : Dealer East : Nil vulnerable

WEST	NORTH	EAST	SOUTH
		2♡ (1)	Pass
2♠ (2)	Pass	3♠	4♣
Dble	Pass	Pass	Pass

(1) Weak, five hearts, 4+ minor
(2) Natural, not forcing

What should West lead from:

♠ 10 9 8 6 3
♡ 6
♢ A K 8
♣ A Q 6 4

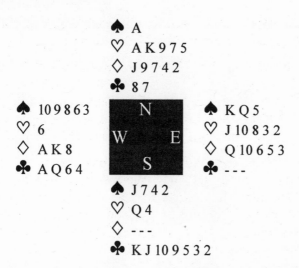

♠ A
♡ A K 9 7 5
◇ J 9 7 4 2
♣ 8 7

♠ 109863
♡ 6
◇ A K 8
♣ A Q 6 4

♠ K Q 5
♡ J 10 8 3 2
◇ Q 10 6 5 3
♣ - - -

♠ J 7 4 2
♡ Q 4
◇ - - -
♣ K J 10 9 5 3 2

Quite a number of tables played in club contracts after various auctions. A few of these were in 4♣ doubled and all but one succeeded. The popular lead was the ◇A and declarer had an easy time.

After ruffing the diamond lead, South played a spade to the ace, heart to the queen, spade ruff, diamond ruff, spade ruff. With the ♠K, ♠Q coming down, South's ♠J was high. After ruffing another diamond South played the ♣K, West won and returned the ♠10. South won and played a heart. West ruffed, but could not score more than three trump tricks. North-South +510.

At the table where 4♣ doubled was defeated, West was the Old Master after the auction opposite. Since he was almost certain to score two club tricks anyway, the Old Master began with the ♣A to take a look at dummy. At trick 2 he switched to the ♡6.

South won with the ♡Q, played a spade to the ace, ruffed a diamond and ruffed a spade. There was no way to prevent the Old Master from scoring a heart ruff. Declarer ruffed a diamond, cashed the ♣K and played the ♣J. West won, played a spade to East, who returned a heart, ruffed. One down.

I also helped the Old Master on this deal, said the club ace.

Imps : Dealer South : North-South vulnerable

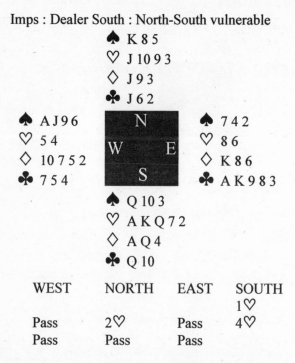

♠ K 8 5
♥ J 10 9 3
♦ J 9 3
♣ J 6 2

♠ A J 9 6
♥ 5 4
♦ 10 7 5 2
♣ 7 5 4

♠ 7 4 2
♥ 8 6
♦ K 8 6
♣ A K 9 8 3

♠ Q 10 3
♥ A K Q 7 2
♦ A Q 4
♣ Q 10

WEST	NORTH	EAST	SOUTH
			1♥
Pass	2♥	Pass	4♥
Pass	Pass	Pass	

West led the ♥4 and South took the ♥A and ♥K, followed by
the ♣Q. West played the ♣7, reverse count, and the Old Master
won with the ♣K. South's club play was almost certainly from
♣Q-10 doubleton and so South was heading for a discard. The
Old Master could see two defensive tricks, but where were two
more? A diamond switch would be right if West had the ♦Q and
the ♠A, but a diamond switch was not needed unless South had a
4-5-2-2 pattern. With the ♦J in dummy, a diamond switch was
risky and would have given South three diamond tricks and the
contract. The Old Master switched to the ♠7: three – nine – king.

Declarer continued with the ♣6 from dummy: ace – ten – five.
Should East continue spades or switch to a diamond?

If South was 4-5-2-2 and West had the ♢A a diamond switch was vital, but if West's winners were in spades, the Old Master had to pursue the spades.

I don't know why you are claiming credit for this deal, said the club five to the club ace. All you did was win the trick. I was the one who gave the Old Master the right message.

What do you mean? asked the heart five.

The big guys are always trying to take credit, replied the club five. You see, after the second round of clubs, only one club was missing. The Old Master knew that his partner had started with ♣7-5-4. Since West chose to play me, the higher of the remaining 5-4, under the ♣A, West was sending a suit-preference message that the solution was in the higher suit. If West had worthless spades and the ♢A, he would have played the ♣4 under the ace.

So the Old Master continued spades? asked the heart five.

Of course, said the club five. 4♡ was defeated for a good swing. At the other table the bidding had been 1♡ : 2♡, 3NT and the ♠6 lead eliminated any problems for declarer. Tsk, that ♣A. I am so ticked off by the such high-handedness.

Now, now, said the spade ace. You do have a point, but there's no need to be worked up about it. By the way, we have not had a tale from you? Do you have a deal other the one just mentioned?

Yes, indeed, I do, said the club five, and it is a salutary lesson to anyone playing against an expert, let alone against the Old Master. If you give a top player gratuitous information, you can expect to pay heavily for it. Here is the deal . . .

Double exposure

The story of the ♣5

Imps : Dealer South : North-South vulnerable

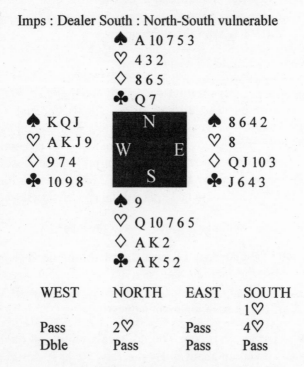

```
              ♠ A 10 7 5 3
              ♡ 4 3 2
              ◇ 8 6 5
              ♣ Q 7
♠ K Q J                        ♠ 8 6 4 2
♡ A K J 9       N              ♡ 8
◇ 9 7 4      W     E           ◇ Q J 10 3
♣ 10 9 8        S              ♣ J 6 4 3
              ♠ 9
              ♡ Q 10 7 6 5
              ◇ A K 2
              ♣ A K 5 2
```

WEST	NORTH	EAST	SOUTH
			1♡
Pass	2♡	Pass	4♡
Dble	Pass	Pass	Pass

No doubt West felt he was on a sure thing when he doubled 4♡, but when the play was over he regretted his action.

West began with the ♠K, taken by the ace. It was clear to the Old Master that West's double had to be based on a trump stack. Accordingly there was no point in touching the trump suit early. After a spade ruff at trick 2 the Old Master played the ♣2 to the ♣Q and cashed the ♣A, ♣K, discarding a diamond from dummy. After ◇A, ◇K, a diamond ruff was followed by another spade ruff, leaving this end-position:

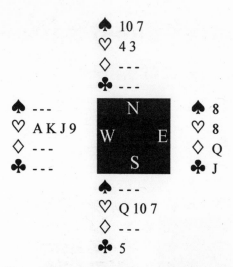

All that remained was for the Old Master to play me, said the club five, and West was restricted to just three trump tricks.

A double certainly can be a dangerous weapon, agreed the heart jack. The same applies when a takeout double is left in for penalties. Consider this problem:

Imps : Dealer East : North-South vulnerable

WEST	NORTH	EAST	SOUTH
		1♣ (1)	1♥
Pass	2♥	Dble (2)	Pass
Pass	Pass		

(1) Artificial, strong, 15+ points
(2) For takeout

For better or worse, West passed the double with:

    ♠ 6 5
    ♥ 8 7 6 5 4
    ◇ Q 8 4
    ♣ K J 2

What would you choose as your opening lead?

Passing fancy? Fancy passing!

The stories of the ♡J

This was the full deal, said the heart jack:

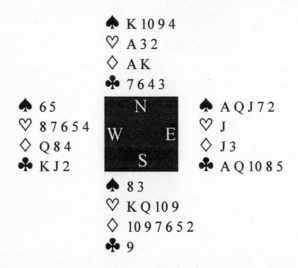

```
              ♠ K 10 9 4
              ♡ A 3 2
              ◇ A K
              ♣ 7 6 4 3
  ♠ 6 5                        ♠ A Q J 7 2
  ♡ 8 7 6 5 4                  ♡ J
  ◇ Q 8 4                      ◇ J 3
  ♣ K J 2                      ♣ A Q 10 8 5
              ♠ 8 3
              ♡ K Q 10 9
              ◇ 10 9 7 6 5 2
              ♣ 9
```

Passing with no trump tricks was a brave or foolhardy move, depending on the outcome. West can beat 2♡ by leading a trump. That is usually the best policy when your side has more strength than the opponents. If declarer wins and cashes the ◇A, ◇K, followed by a low club, East ducks – and the Old Master would have done that. West wins and a second trump will defeat 2♡.

Alas, West led the ♠6: ten – jack. East played off the ♣A and continued with the ♣5. South ruffed and cashed the ◇A, ◇K. After ruffing another club to hand, South played a third diamond and ruffed the ◇Q with the ♡2. East gratefully over-ruffed with the ♡J and played another club. South ruffed and played the ◇10. West ruffed and dummy over-ruffed with the ♡A, but South now had to go one down. West was thus saved from his passing folly.

Shouldn't declarer make 2♡ doubled? asked the diamond nine.

Definitely after that opening lead, said the heart jack. After East wins with the ♡J, cashes the ♣A and plays the ♣5, South should ruff, cash the ◇A, ◇K, play a spade to the king and now can ruff a diamond low. After another club ruff, declarer ruffs a diamond high and scores two diamonds and six trump tricks.

I featured in another pretty deal, said the heart jack, but I was not with the Old Master. I was against him and everyone predicted that his contract could not be made. Even I thought the contract was doomed, but why not look at it first as a declarer problem?

Teams : South dealer : North-South vulnerable

> NORTH
> ♠ 7 3
> ♡ Q 9 7 5 3
> ◇ A 8 3
> ♣ A 7 3
>
> SOUTH
> ♠ A K 10 6 2
> ♡ A 8
> ◇ 6 5 2
> ♣ K J 9

WEST	NORTH	EAST	SOUTH
			1NT
Pass	2◇ (1)	Dble	Pass
Pass	Rdbl	Pass	2♡
Pass	3◇	Pass	3♠
Pass	4♡	All pass	

(1) Transfer to hearts

West leads the ◇9. How would you plan the play?

Heart bypass operation

The second story of the ♡J

South dealer : North-South vulnerable

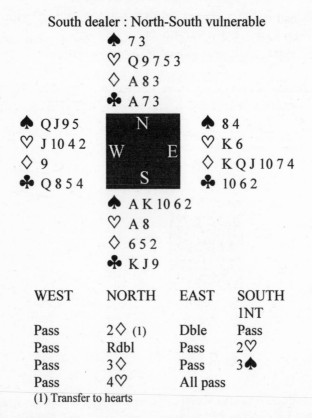

```
                    ♠ 73
                    ♡ Q 9 7 5 3
                    ◇ A 8 3
                    ♣ A 7 3
♠ Q J 9 5          N          ♠ 8 4
♡ J 10 4 2    W         E     ♡ K 6
◇ 9                          ◇ K Q J 10 7 4
♣ Q 8 5 4          S          ♣ 10 6 2
                    ♠ A K 10 6 2
                    ♡ A 8
                    ◇ 6 5 2
                    ♣ K J 9
```

WEST	NORTH	EAST	SOUTH
			1NT
Pass	2◇ (1)	Dble	Pass
Pass	Rdbl	Pass	2♡
Pass	3◇	Pass	3♠
Pass	4♡	All pass	

(1) Transfer to hearts

East doubled to show strong diamonds and North redoubled to ask South to take the transfer. North's 3◇ asked for a diamond stopper. 3♠ showed spades and denied help in diamonds.

In the semi-finals of the 2003 World Championships some played in 3NT, which succeeded. When the Old Master reached 4♡, no one thought it could be made on a diamond lead. How little they knew.

As you can see declarer could lose two or three hearts, not to mention a club and a diamond or two, said the heart jack.

So tell us what happened!

West did lead the ◇9 and the Old Master took it with the ace. To try to keep East off lead, he played the ♡3 and covered East's six with his eight. West won and switched to the ♠Q.

The Old Master won with the ♠A, cashed the ♡A, dropping the king, and continued with the ♠K and a spade ruff. This was now the position:

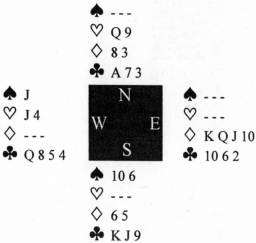

The Old Master was still staring at a heart loser, a club loser and two diamond losers and West was looking pretty happy with himself. That is, until the Old Master played the ♡Q, followed by the ♡9, discarding both his diamonds. I won, of course, said the heart jack, but what could West do? He could cash the ♠J, but the forced club exit gave the Old Master the rest of the tricks. Had he played a club without cashing the ♠J, the Old Master would win and play another spade himself.

On your deal, said the diamond nine, the Old Master used the trump suit for a throw-in play. On this deal the Old Master used me for the same purpose, and he did without drawing all of the trumps first. Here is the deal . . .

A happy ending

The story of the ◇9

Dealer South : East-West vulnerable

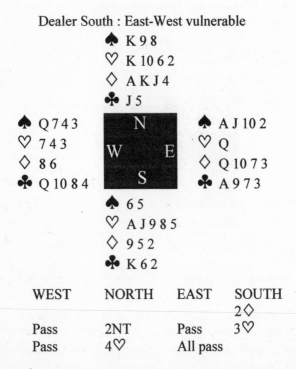

	♠ K 9 8	
	♡ K 10 6 2	
	◇ A K J 4	
	♣ J 5	

♠ Q 7 4 3		♠ A J 10 2
♡ 7 4 3		♡ Q
◇ 8 6		◇ Q 10 7 3
♣ Q 10 8 4		♣ A 9 7 3

	♠ 6 5	
	♡ A J 9 8 5	
	◇ 9 5 2	
	♣ K 6 2	

WEST	NORTH	EAST	SOUTH
			2◇
Pass	2NT	Pass	3♡
Pass	4♡	All pass	

The 2◇ opening was a multi, a weak two with a 5- or 6-card suit. 2NT was a strong inquiry and 3♡ showed a maximum, but only five hearts. That did not deter North from raising to game. West started with the ♣4. Had he started with any other suit, the outcome might have been different.

The Old Master played the ♣J from dummy and East took the
♣A. The ♣K won the ♣3 return and the third club was ruffed.
The ♡K came next and the ♡Q from East was a welcome sight.

The Old Master continued with the ♡2 to his ace. Then came
my big moment, said the diamond nine. At trick 5, the Old Master
played me. When West followed with the ◇6, I thought for sure
that I would be covered by one of dummy's honours, but no, the
Old Master played dummy's ◇4. East won with the ◇10 and this
was the ending:

```
              ♠ K 9 8
              ♡ 10
              ◇ A K J
              ♣ - - -
♠ Q 7 4 3      N        ♠ A J 10
♡ 7                     ♡ - - -
◇ 8         W     E     ◇ Q 7 3
♣ Q            S        ♣ 9
              ♠ 6 5
              ♡ J 9 8
              ◇ 5 2
              ♣ - - -
```

There was nothing East could do. The ♣9 would give declarer a
ruff-and-discard. A diamond return into dummy's tenace would
allow declarer to draw the missing trump and then discard a spade
on dummy's last diamond. Either way declarer would lose only
one spade and a spade play by East would have the same effect.

I like that deal, said the spade six. It is always a pleasure to see
players make use of the lower cards to achieve their objective.
The honours deserve to take most of the tricks, I suppose, but
when we lower cards come into play, that is a delight. Have a look
at this deal, where the Old Master used me to good advantage.

You sixy thing

The story of the ♠6

Dealer West : Nil vulnerable

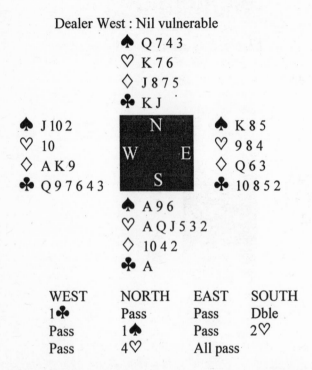

	♠ Q 7 4 3		
	♡ K 7 6		
	◇ J 8 7 5		
	♣ K J		

♠ J 10 2		♠ K 8 5
♡ 10		♡ 9 8 4
◇ A K 9		◇ Q 6 3
♣ Q 9 7 6 4 3		♣ 10 8 5 2

	♠ A 9 6
	♡ A Q J 5 3 2
	◇ 10 4 2
	♣ A

WEST	NORTH	EAST	SOUTH
1♣	Pass	Pass	Dble
Pass	1♠	Pass	2♡
Pass	4♡	All pass	

West started with the ◇A, but could not afford to continue
diamonds, else declarer would have two spade discards later on
the ♣K and the thirteenth diamond. West switched to the ♠J:
queen – king – ace. The Old Master cashed the ♡A, ♡Q and
unblocked the ♣A. A heart to the king drew East's last trump and
the ♣K allowed declarer to discard a losing diamond.

Next came the ♠3: five and the Old Master finessed me, said
the spade six. That forced out the ♠10 and made the ♠9 high for
the game-going trick.

You were lucky to be able to force out an honour, said the heart four. It's hard for us low cards to score tricks, but we can be very useful in other ways. Have a look at how I helped the Old Master:

Showtime

The story of the ♡4

Dealer South : Nil vulnerable

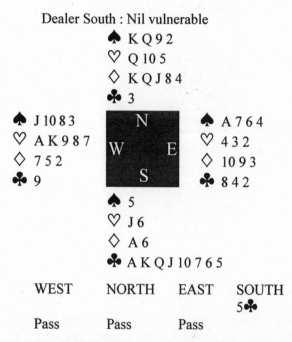

```
              ♠ K Q 9 2
              ♡ Q 10 5
              ◇ K Q J 8 4
              ♣ 3
♠ J 10 8 3                      ♠ A 7 6 4
♡ A K 9 8 7      N             ♡ 4 3 2
◇ 7 5 2        W   E           ◇ 10 9 3
♣ 9              S             ♣ 8 4 2
              ♠ 5
              ♡ J 6
              ◇ A 6
              ♣ A K Q J 10 7 6 5
```

WEST	NORTH	EAST	SOUTH
			5♣
Pass	Pass	Pass	

West began with the ♡A and the Old Master played the ♡2 to show an odd number of hearts. Even though South dropped the ♡J, West knew South had another heart. West cashed the ♡K and my moment had come, said the heart four. When the Old Master played me, West knew this was the higher of the remaining ♡4-3. That indicated a desire for the high suit and when West shifted to a spade, the contract was one down. Any other suit at trick 3 and South would have made the game.

You should not be so hard on us, said the heart five. You might be surprised at the power we small chaps can wield. Why, I recall when I was the one drawing trumps on the third round of the suit. This was the deal . . .

Count me out

The story of the ♡5

Dealer West : East-West vulnerable

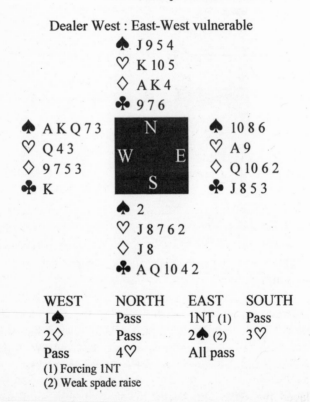

```
                        ♠ J 9 5 4
                        ♡ K 10 5
                        ◇ A K 4
                        ♣ 9 7 6
♠ A K Q 7 3        N              ♠ 10 8 6
♡ Q 4 3      W         E          ♡ A 9
◇ 9 7 5 3                         ◇ Q 10 6 2
♣ K                S              ♣ J 8 5 3
                        ♠ 2
                        ♡ J 8 7 6 2
                        ◇ J 8
                        ♣ A Q 10 4 2
```

WEST	NORTH	EAST	SOUTH
1♠	Pass	1NT (1)	Pass
2◇	Pass	2♠ (2)	3♡
Pass	4♡	All pass	

(1) Forcing 1NT
(2) Weak spade raise

West led the ♠A and continued with the ♠K at trick 2. The Old Master ruffed and played the ♡J: queen – king – ace. East returned a spade, again ruffed.

Down to ♡8-7 the Old Master did not want to risk losing a deep
heart finesse and perhaps East returning a third heart. Accordingly
he played the ♡7 to dummy's ten and the ♡9 dropped. The
fourth spade was ruffed, as East discarded a diamond. This was
now the position:

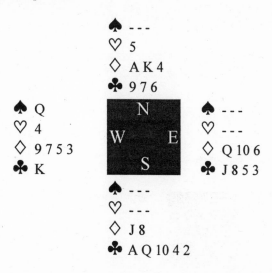

```
                  ♠ - - -
                  ♡ 5
                  ◇ A K 4
                  ♣ 9 7 6
  ♠ Q                          ♠ - - -
  ♡ 4          N               ♡ - - -
  ◇ 9 7 5 3  W     E           ◇ Q 10 6
  ♣ K          S               ♣ J 8 5 3
                  ♠ - - -
                  ♡ - - -
                  ◇ J 8
                  ♣ A Q 10 4 2
```

There I was, continued the heart five, the top trump, and just as
good as those high and mighty aces that always look down on us.
The Old Master played the ◇ J, three from West, and overtook it
in dummy. I came next and removed West's trump. East threw a
diamond and South a club.

The Old Master paused to put the pieces together for the
opposing hands. West's failure to cover the ◇ J indicated the ◇Q
was with East, who had already shown up with the ♡A. With the
♣K as well, East would be too strong for a weak raise to 2♠.

Having placed the ♣K with West, the Old Master continued
with the ♣6 to the ace, felling the king. A diamond to dummy
was followed by the ♣9, jack, queen. The ♣10 was cashed and
East took the last trick with the ♣8.

Using a forcing 1NT response, might not West have started with a 5-3-3-2 pattern with three diamonds? asked the club ten. In that case the ♣K would not fall under the ace.

True, replied the heart five, but after the ♣A, South can simply continue with a low club. As long as the ♣K is with West, the contract will succeed.

Yes, I like it, when you must use logic to find the winning move. East did not manage it on this deal. Would you have done better?

Fair game

The story of the ♣10

Dealer East : North-South vulnerable

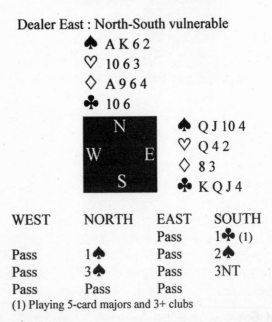

    ♠ A K 6 2
    ♡ 10 6 3
    ◇ A 9 6 4
    ♣ 10 6

    ♠ Q J 10 4
    ♡ Q 4 2
    ◇ 8 3
    ♣ K Q J 4

WEST	NORTH	EAST	SOUTH
		Pass	1♣ (1)
Pass	1♠	Pass	2♠
Pass	3♠	Pass	3NT
Pass	Pass	Pass	

(1) Playing 5-card majors and 3+ clubs

West leads the ♠5: two – queen – seven. East shifts to the ♣K: two – nine (high-encouraging) – six. What should East play next?

If West is encouraging with ♣A-9-x, said the spade ace, then it is vital for East to continue with the ♣4.

But what if West has played the ♣9 from ♣9-8-x-x? In that case East must play a top club next, said the diamond ace.

Obviously East cannot do both, so which one is it? I cannot tell, said the heart eight.

Against the Old Master East failed to make the winning move, said the club ten. The result was that I won trick 3. The full deal:

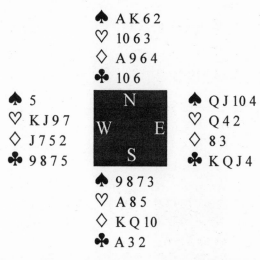

```
                    ♠ A K 6 2
                    ♡ 10 6 3
                    ◇ A 9 6 4
                    ♣ 10 6
  ♠ 5              ┌─────────┐      ♠ Q J 10 4
  ♡ K J 9 7        │    N    │      ♡ Q 4 2
  ◇ J 7 5 2        │ W     E │      ◇ 8 3
  ♣ 9 8 7 5        │    S    │      ♣ K Q J 4
                   └─────────┘
                    ♠ 9 8 7 3
                    ♡ A 8 5
                    ◇ K Q 10
                    ♣ A 3 2
```

After the ♠5 lead, ducked to East, and the ♣K at trick 2, East played the ♣4 next. The Old Master played low and I won the trick. When the ♠A revealed the bad split, the Old Master placed West with a 1-4-4-4 pattern. With a 5+ suit West would probably have led that. After the ◇K, ◇Q, the Old Master played the ◇10 and let it run. He now had two spades, one heart, four diamonds and two clubs.

If West had ♣A-9-x, South has four clubs. With a 3-3-3-4 South would hardly raise 1♠ to 2♠ and with four spades – four clubs, South has a doubleton and would prefer 4♠ to 3NT.

South's suggestion of 3NT after 3♠ strongly suggests a 4-3-3-3 pattern with four spades. That gives West four clubs and East should continue with the ♣Q at trick 3.

Quite right, too, said the club queen. Whether I have the support of the ♣K or not, it is often best to play me. The failure to do so can often be a mistake. Look what happened here . . .

The king and I

The story of the ♣Q

North dealer : East-West vulnerable

```
                    ♠ 5 3
                    ♡ Q J 2
                    ♢ K Q 10 7 6 4
                    ♣ A 4
     ♠ 10 7 4 2         N          ♠ Q 9 8
     ♡ A 7 6 3                     ♡ K 4
     ♢ J             W       E     ♢ 8 3 2
     ♣ J 9 7 3         S          ♣ K Q 10 8 6
                    ♠ A K J 6
                    ♡ 10 9 8 5
                    ♢ A 9 5
                    ♣ 5 2
```

WEST	NORTH	EAST	SOUTH
	1♢	Pass	1♡
Pass	2♢	Pass	2♠
Pass	4♡	All pass	

A more delicate auction would have finished in 3NT, but both tables in a national teams final finished in 4♡.

At both tables the lead was the ♣3, taken by the ace. Declarer played the ♡Q, covered by the king. Both Easts continued by cashing the ♣K, a big error as it turned out.

One East then played the ♡4. Had West ducked this, a diamond ruff ensues if declarer discontinues hearts. If South plays a third heart, West takes the ace and can force declarer by continuing clubs. The position was unclear to West, who took the ♡A and shifted to the ◇J. Declarer won, drew trumps and ran the diamonds.

The other East shifted to the ♠8 at trick 4. Declarer took the ♠A and led a second heart. West played low and the ♡J won. West won the third heart with the ♡A and also tried the ◇J in the hope of a ruff. South won, drew the missing trump and claimed.

A most important aspect of defence is to make life easy for partner, said the club queen. Neither East did that, yet how simple it is. After taking the ♡K at trick 2, all East needs to do is cash me instead of my consort, the club king. That makes the position clear to partner, who will duck the next heart. If declarer tries a third heart, West takes the ♡A and continues clubs for at least a two-trick set. If declarer abandons trumps, West scores a ruff, one down.

Now try this problem, said the club queen. After 2NT : 6NT West leads the ♡9. How would you plan the play?

NORTH
♠ Q J 3
♡ Q J 5
◇ A J 10 7 4
♣ Q 10

SOUTH
♠ A K 5
♡ A K 2
◇ K 6 2
♣ A 7 4 3

Duck be a lady tonight

The second story of the ♣Q

South dealer : Both vulnerable

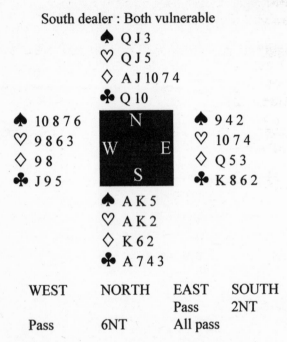

```
              ♠ Q J 3
              ♡ Q J 5
              ◇ A J 10 7 4
              ♣ Q 10

♠ 10 8 7 6      N       ♠ 9 4 2
♡ 9 8 6 3               ♡ 10 7 4
◇ 9 8        W     E    ◇ Q 5 3
♣ J 9 5         S       ♣ K 8 6 2

              ♠ A K 5
              ♡ A K 2
              ◇ K 6 2
              ♣ A 7 4 3
```

WEST	NORTH	EAST	SOUTH
		Pass	2NT
Pass	6NT	All pass	

West led the ♡9. As declarer has seven tricks outside diamonds you want to bring in five diamond tricks. The normal play would be ◇K and finesse the ◇J. That caters for a singleton ◇Q or West having Q-x, Q-x-x or Q-x-x-x. If you suspected East holding the ◇Q, you can cross to dummy and lead the ◇J. This is not as good a chance, as you cannot pick up Q-x-x-x with East and there are no strong grounds to place the ◇Q with East here.

The diamond ace interjected, So, if declarer played the diamonds normally, 6NT was one down?

No, replied the club queen, because South was the Old Master.

He took the ♡9 lead in dummy and played me at trick 2, said the club queen. If the normal play in diamonds would yield five tricks it would still do so later. In the meantime playing me gave the Old Master an extra chance. Put yourself in East's position. To cover with the ♣K might set up a long club suit for South. By ducking you ensure a trick for yourself with the ♣K later.

Accordingly East played low and I won the trick, the club queen continued. With the extra trick in clubs the Old Master needed only four tricks from the diamonds and he claimed when all followed to the ◇K.

That was pretty neat, said the diamond ace. I have a couple of situations I'd like to share with you. Here is the first:

North dealer : Nil vulnerable

```
            NORTH
            ♠ A 8 7 3
            ♡ 4
            ◇ K Q 9 8 2
            ♣ A K 9


            SOUTH
            ♠ K Q J 6 4 2
            ♡ A J 10 5 3
            ◇ 6 3
            ♣ - - -
```

WEST	NORTH	EAST	SOUTH
	1♣ (1)	2NT (2)	3♠
5♣	5♠	Pass	6♠
Pass	Pass	Pass	

(1) Artificial, 16+ points
(2) Weak, both minors

West leads the ◇J. How should South plan the play?

Dupe du jour

The story of the ♦A

North dealer : Nil vulnerable

```
              ♠ A 8 7 3
              ♥ 4
              ♦ K Q 9 8 2
              ♣ A K 9
♠ 9 5            N            ♠ 10
♥ K 8 7 6 2   W     E        ♥ Q 9
♦ J              S            ♦ A 10 7 5 4
♣ Q J 8 6 3                  ♣ 10 7 5 4 2
              ♠ K Q J 6 4 2
              ♥ A J 10 5 3
              ♦ 6 3
              ♣ - - -
```

South was in 6♠ after East had shown both minors. West led the ♦J. It was clear to South that the lead was a singleton and so he ducked in dummy. The hope was that East would also play low and South's other diamond would vanish on a top club later.

It was not to be, said the diamond ace. The Old Master, East, covered the ♦J with me and returned a diamond. It is not easy to dupe the Old Master . . . Now consider this problem:

East dealer : Nil vulnerable				West to lead from:
WEST	NORTH	EAST	SOUTH	♠ - - -
		Pass	1♠	♥ Q 8 5
2NT*	4♠	5♦	Dble**	♦ A J 9 5 3
Pass	5♠	All pass		♣ Q J 8 4 3
*Minors **Penalties				

Leading to disaster

The second story of the ♦ A

East dealer : Nil vulnerable

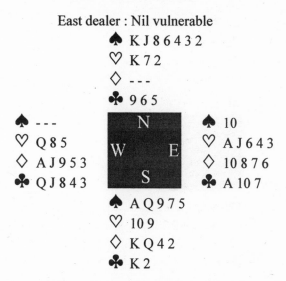

♠ K J 8 6 4 3 2
♡ K 7 2
♦ - - -
♣ 9 6 5

♠ - - -
♡ Q 8 5
♦ A J 9 5 3
♣ Q J 8 4 3

♠ 10
♡ A J 6 4 3
♦ 10 8 7 6
♣ A 10 7

♠ A Q 9 7 5
♡ 10 9
♦ K Q 4 2
♣ K 2

Although the Old Master's double of 5♦ was for penalties, North felt the shape was too extreme and so removed to 5♠. That turned out to be a good decision for a number of reasons. Firstly, 5♦ can be made if declarer picks the position in both red suits. Secondly, West led the only card to allow 5♠ to make.

He led me, said the diamond ace, despite South's double of 5♦. Not a good idea. The Old Master ruffed the lead, drew the missing trump with the ♠A and discarded two hearts from dummy. Now he lost only one heart and one club.

The lead was poor, the spade ace agreed, but East might have been more helpful. East might have doubled 5♠ as a warning to West not to lead a diamond. Whether West leads a heart or a club, South has no hope of making the contract. I had a similar experience myself, said the spade ace . . .

Lead turns to lead

The story of the ♠A

West dealer : Both vulnerable

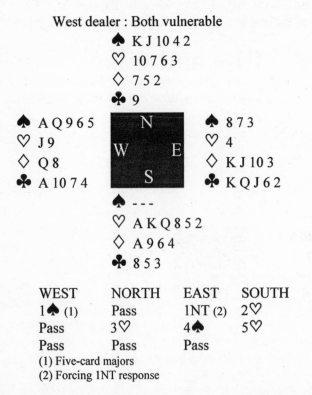

```
              ♠ K J 10 4 2
              ♡ 10 7 6 3
              ◇ 7 5 2
              ♣ 9

♠ A Q 9 6 5        N           ♠ 8 7 3
♡ J 9          W       E       ♡ 4
◇ Q 8              S           ◇ K J 10 3
♣ A 10 7 4                     ♣ K Q J 6 2

              ♠ - - -
              ♡ A K Q 8 5 2
              ◇ A 9 6 4
              ♣ 8 5 3
```

WEST	NORTH	EAST	SOUTH
1♠ (1)	Pass	1NT (2)	2♡
Pass	3♡	4♠	5♡
Pass	Pass	Pass	

(1) Five-card majors
(2) Forcing 1NT response

West began with me, said the spade ace. Granted West had a tough choice, but leading out aces in trump contracts is the stuff screams are made of. The Old Master ruffed low, cashed the ♡A and then led the ♣3. West went in with the ♣10 and East played low. Having started poorly, West continued, fatally, with the ♡J, whereas a diamond switch was needed.

The Old Master won, ruffed a club and discarded a diamond on the ♠K. Another diamond went on the ♠J and that was that.

West won with the ♠Q, but there were no more tricks for the defence. West shifted to the ◇Q (finally). The Old Master won, ruffed his last club and pitched his remaining diamond on the ♠10.

It is a wise player who knows when to take an ace. The Old Master found the best use for me on this deal, said the spade ace . . .

Rise and shine

The second story of the ♠A

North dealer : North-South vulnerable

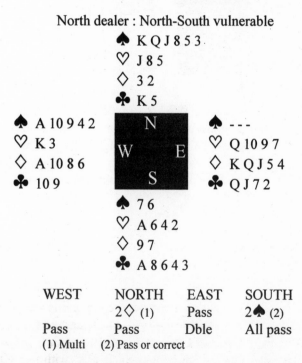

```
            ♠ K Q J 8 5 3
            ♡ J 8 5
            ◇ 3 2
            ♣ K 5
♠ A 10 9 4 2              ♠ - - -
♡ K 3         N          ♡ Q 10 9 7
◇ A 10 8 6  W   E        ◇ K Q J 5 4
♣ 10 9        S          ♣ Q J 7 2
            ♠ 7 6
            ♡ A 6 4 2
            ◇ 9 7
            ♣ A 8 6 4 3
```

WEST	NORTH	EAST	SOUTH
	2◇ (1)	Pass	2♠ (2)
Pass	Pass	Dble	All pass
(1) Multi	(2) Pass or correct		

South's 2♠ showed good support for hearts, but not for spades. West led the ♡K, taken by the ace. The ♠7 came next, ten, jack, ◇5. After ♣K, club to the ace, South played the ♠6. How do you think West should defend?

This was the position when South led the ♣6:

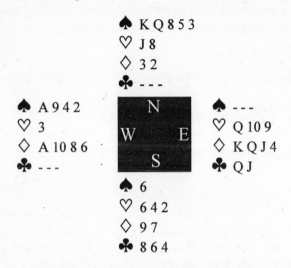

The Old Master rose with the ♠A (the spade ace liked to speak of himself from time to time in the third person) and continued with the ♡3. East won and cashed another heart. Then came the ◊K, followed by the ◊Q. That removed all of North's cards bar the trumps. East played the fourth heart, ruffed in dummy, but with North holding ♠K-Q-8 the Old Master with ♠9-4-2 scored the ♠9 for the setting trick.

Suppose the Old Master had played low on the ♣6. Declarer would follow low in dummy and retain the lead. Now a club from South ensures six trump tricks for declarer whatever West does.

It would not help West to play the ♠9 on South's ♠6. Dummy wins and can simply draw trumps after knocking out the ♠A. The only defence to beat 2♠ doubled was to rise with me, said the spade ace. That gives you an idea of how tough it is to defend at a low level when one defender is void in trumps.

Quiet, I hear someone coming, said the heart queen . . .

Walter Zettner came into the room. He walked very slowly, his cane supporting his weight. He had been to the information desk on the ground floor to ask for the Old Master's room.

"Mr. Master's room, please?"

"Mr. O. Master?"

"Yes, that's right."

"That will be level 13, room 7, South wing."

'7S, level 13,' thought Zettner, as he made for the lifts. 'How apt.'

Zettner sat quietly by the Old Master's bed. He looked at all the tubes, hooked up to the Old Master. The various monitors beeped softly. He sat there deep in thought for more than forty minutes as he held the Old Master's hand. There was no response and a tear trickled slowly down Zettner's cheek. He got up, went to the bedside, kissed the Old Master on the forehead and left.

When there are visitors, it is best for us not to continue, said the heart queen. The Old Master might be able to sense the presence of the visitor and that might also be of help. Anyway, it is all right to go on now. Who's next?

I have just remembered another problem, which might amuse you, said the spade six. Here is the bidding:

WEST	NORTH	EAST	SOUTH
	1♡	Pass	2♢
Pass	3♡	Pass	4NT
Pass	5♣ (1)	Pass	5♢ (2)
Pass	5♠ (3)	Pass	5NT (4)
Pass	6♡ (5)	Pass	7NT
Pass	Pass	Pass	

(1) 0 or 3 key cards for hearts   (2) Asking for the ♡Q
(3) 'I have it.'   (4) Asking for specific kings   (5) None outside hearts

West to lead from:

     ♠ K J 7 6 4 3   ♡ J 4 3   ♢ 9   ♣ 8 4 3

Forthright

The second story of the ♠6

You have a great memory, said the spade queen, I remember this deal, too, but it happened a long time ago, on Christmas day in Santa Fe, well before Jenny and the Old Master were married.

That's right, said the spade six. This was the complete deal:

North dealer : Both vulnerable

```
                    ♠ A 10
                    ♡ A K Q 8 6 2
                    ◊ 5 4
                    ♣ J 10 5
 ♠ K J 7 6 4 3              ♠ 8 5
 ♡ J 4 3          N         ♡ 10 9 7 5
 ◊ 9           W     E      ◊ J 10 6 3 2
 ♣ 8 4 3          S         ♣ 7 2
                    ♠ Q 9 2
                    ♡ - - -
                    ◊ A K Q 8 7
                    ♣ A K Q 9 6
```

Jenny had just finished a course of beginners' classes. She proudly told the Old Master she could now play bridge and there was no reason why they should not play together. Amused, the Old Master agreed and this deal arose on their first bridge date.

After the opponents had bid to 7NT by South, Jenny chose me as her opening lead, said the spade six. You can see the dilemma South faced. No one, but no one would lead away from a king against a grand slam and so South rose with the ♠A.

That was the end of the grand slam. South cashed three clubs, staying in dummy, as the Old Master threw a spade. Then came the top hearts, South ditching a diamond and two spades, but nothing good happened and at the end the Old Master took trick thirteen with the ♢J.

"That was a very successful lead, darling," said the Old Master.

"It was obvious," replied Jenny. "Our teacher taught us that against no-trumps, you lead fourth of your longest and strongest suit."

"Fourth was certainly right this time," agreed the Old Master. "Declarer had to believe that I had the ♠K. The ♠A was a vital entry to dummy and your lead stopped me from being squeezed."

"Oh, I'll make up for that later," Jenny said with a demure smile.

The opponents were none too happy about the result, said the heart ten. North blamed South for not ducking the opening lead and South retorted that anyone can play well with 20/20 hindsight. North went on that 7♣ would have been laydown. It's such a pity that humans cannot be kind to each other.

I remember another grand slam, which involved Jenny, the heart ten continued, but this time her partner was not the Old Master. Jenny was still only just out of her beginners' classes and was playing in a supervised session for novices. With neither side vulnerable, she opened 3♡ as dealer with:

♠ 3
♡ A Q J 8 7 6 2
♢ 5
♣ 8 6 4 3

It went pass, pass, double, pass, pass and her partner now bid 4♢. Right hand-opponent doubled this. What would you do if you held Jenny's cards? Decide before looking at the complete deal . . .

The grand opening

The story of the ♡10

South dealer : Nil vulnerable

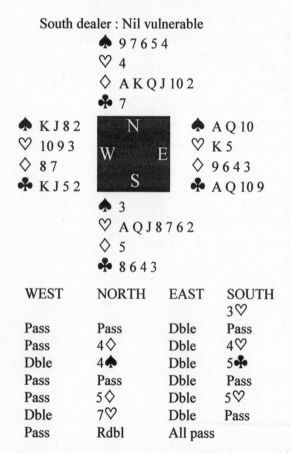

```
                ♠ 97654
                ♡ 4
                ◇ AKQJ102
                ♣ 7
♠ KJ82                        ♠ AQ10
♡ 1093          N            ♡ K5
◇ 87          W   E          ◇ 9643
♣ KJ52          S            ♣ AQ109
                ♠ 3
                ♡ AQJ8762
                ◇ 5
                ♣ 8643
```

WEST	NORTH	EAST	SOUTH
			3♡
Pass	Pass	Dble	Pass
Pass	4◇	Dble	4♡
Dble	4♠	Dble	5♣
Pass	Pass	Dble	Pass
Pass	5◇	Dble	5♡
Dble	7♡	Dble	Pass
Pass	Rdbl	All pass	

None of the combatants had been playing long. West thought East's takeout double of 3♡ was actually for penalties and passed. North tried a rescue move to 4◇. East, thinking West was strong in hearts, figured that he had plenty of defensive values even if they were not in diamonds and doubled 4◇. Jenny returned to 4♡.

If East can double 3♡, I can double 4♡, thought West, and now North tried a second rescue to 4♠. East had no trouble doubling that. Unaware of North's intentions, Jenny ran to 5♣, passed by West and, happy to play anywhere undoubled, North also passed.

Not so East, who doubled with even more confidence. Judging her hearts to be considerably better than her clubs, Jenny reverted to 5♡. North finally snapped and in a fit of pique raised to 7♡. When East's double came back to him, North redoubled. In trade talk this is known as a retribution redouble. North was intent on teaching South a lesson she would not forget.

The spotlight now fell on West, said the heart ten. He had to find an opening lead. With every suit bid by North-South, West was anxious not to give a trick away with the lead. A diamond was particularly unappealing, since that seemed to be dummy's best suit. He remembered a piece of advice he had heard from one of his other partners: 'Against a grand slam a trump is the safest lead.'

A trump could hardly be wrong here, thought West. After all East had doubled 3♡. With an air of confidence he placed me on the table, said the heart ten. The play from that point did not take very long. Jenny captured East's ♡K and drew the missing trumps. A diamond to dummy allowed her to discard all her black losers. That was 7♡ doubled, redoubled and made.

"Couldn't you lead something else?" said East. "Anything but a trump would have beaten the contract."

****

Did you see that? said the heart queen.

What do you mean? asked the heart ten.

I'm sure a brief smile appeared on the Old Master's face. Pity there was no one in the room to see it.

Maybe that story was helpful, said the heart ten. I have another where I was of use to Jenny, but it took place many years later.

End insight

The second story of the ♡10

North dealer : Both vulnerable

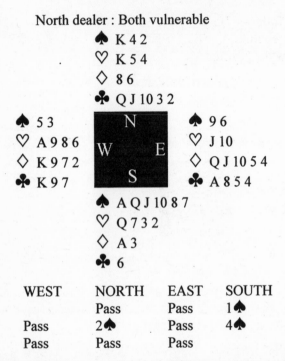

```
                    ♠ K 4 2
                    ♡ K 5 4
                    ◇ 8 6
                    ♣ Q J 10 3 2
    ♠ 5 3              N              ♠ 9 6
    ♡ A 9 8 6     W         E         ♡ J 10
    ◇ K 9 7 2         S              ◇ Q J 10 5 4
    ♣ K 9 7                           ♣ A 8 5 4
                    ♠ A Q J 10 8 7
                    ♡ Q 7 3 2
                    ◇ A 3
                    ♣ 6
```

WEST	NORTH	EAST	SOUTH
	Pass	Pass	1♠
Pass	2♠	Pass	4♠
Pass	Pass	Pass	

When the Old Master raised to 2♠, Jenny followed one of the precepts she had learned from him: 'If we have a 9-card trump fit or better and one of us has ten or more cards in two suits, bid game.' Hence Jenny jumped to 4♠ over 2♠.

West began with the ◇2. Jenny surveyed the dummy. Prospects did not look good. A club loser was inevitable and likewise now a diamond. That meant that she could afford only one heart loser. That was not likely. Perhaps if an opponent held ace-doubleton in hearts? Even if that layout existed, and as you can see it did not, then declarer had to deal with the fourth round of hearts.

The ◇2 lead went to the ten and ace and Jenny played the ♣6:
seven – queen – ace. East cashed the ◇Q and then shifted to the
♡J: two – six – king. A low club was ruffed, followed by the ♠A
and the ♠8 to the ♠K.

When all followed to the second spade, Jenny saw a faint
chance. She continued with another low club and the ♣K fell.
This was now the position:

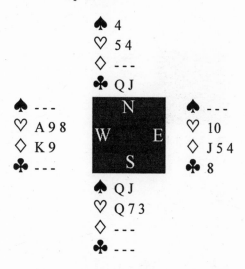

Jenny exited with the ♡3. This would work perfectly if either
East or West had started with ace-doubleton, but it also worked on
the actual layout. It would not help West to rise with the ♡A and
when he played low, I won the trick, said the heart ten. East was
left with only minor suit cards. No matter which he played, Jenny
had the rest of the tricks.

In practice East played a diamond. Jenny ruffed in hand and
discarded dummy's remaining heart. Dummy's cards were all high.

Success via an endplay is always elegant, said the spade three. I
was involved in one, but only due to an opponent's decision . . .

Coup du jour

The story of the ♠3

East dealer : Nil vulnerable

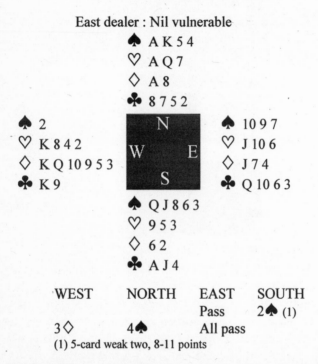

```
                    ♠ A K 5 4
                    ♡ A Q 7
                    ◇ A 8
                    ♣ 8 7 5 2
♠ 2                                      ♠ 10 9 7
♡ K 8 4 2           N                    ♡ J 10 6
◇ K Q 10 9 5 3    W   E                  ◇ J 7 4
♣ K 9               S                    ♣ Q 10 6 3
                    ♠ Q J 8 6 3
                    ♡ 9 5 3
                    ◇ 6 2
                    ♣ A J 4
```

WEST	NORTH	EAST	SOUTH
		Pass	2♠ (1)
3◇	4♠	All pass	

(1) 5-card weak two, 8-11 points

While 3NT would have been easy to make, one cannot quarrel with North's decision to raise to 4♠. West began with the ◇K, ducked in dummy. East played the ◇4, showing an odd number. The Old Master always felt comfortable playing against those who gave count religiously. It made the counting of the hand much easier.

West played a second diamond and the Old Master drew trumps with the ♠A, ♠K and the ♠4 to his queen. He was careful to keep me in his hand, said the spade three, and he followed with the ♠6 and ♠8. Meanwhile West discarded two diamonds.

When a heart to the queen held, the Old Master cashed the ♡A, leaving these cards:

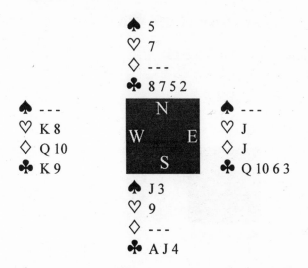

He exited with dummy's ♡7 and West allowed East's ♡J to hold. When East switched to the ♣3, the Old Master rose with the ♣A. Seeing the endplay looming, West ditched the ♣K, but that did not help. This is where the Old Master had seen how I might still be necessary, said the spade three. He led me to dummy's ♠5 and played the next club from dummy. East could take the ♣Q, but the ♣J was the tenth trick for declarer.

Of course, it became your story only after West jettisoned me, said the club king. If West had kept me in his hand, this would have become the story of the ♣4 or the ♣J.

I noted that you mentioned how helpful count cards by the defenders can be for declarer, the club king went on. Working out the shape of the hands is vital of course, but the strength of an opponent's hand can also be a vital clue. The Old Master had no problem on this deal . . .

Counter productive

The story of the ♣K

South dealer : Both vulnerable

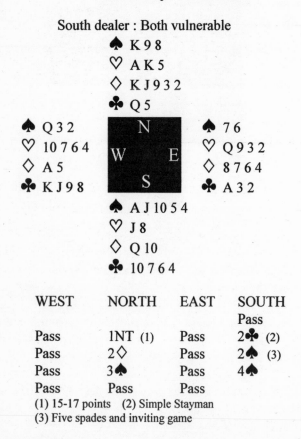

```
                        ♠ K 9 8
                        ♡ A K 5
                        ◇ K J 9 3 2
                        ♣ Q 5

    ♠ Q 3 2              N              ♠ 7 6
    ♡ 10 7 6 4                          ♡ Q 9 3 2
    ◇ A 5        W              E       ◇ 8 7 6 4
    ♣ K J 9 8           S              ♣ A 3 2

                        ♠ A J 10 5 4
                        ♡ J 8
                        ◇ Q 10
                        ♣ 10 7 6 4
```

WEST	NORTH	EAST	SOUTH
			Pass
Pass	1NT (1)	Pass	2♣ (2)
Pass	2◇	Pass	2♠ (3)
Pass	3♠	Pass	4♠
Pass	Pass	Pass	

(1) 15-17 points   (2) Simple Stayman
(3) Five spades and inviting game

The Old Master led the ♡4, taken by the ace. East played the
♡2, low-like. The ◇2 came next: four (bottom from an even
number) – queen – ace. The Old Master continued with the ♡6,
won by the king. Declarer tackled trumps with the ♠K, followed
by the ♠9 which was run to West's queen. A lesser player might
play a third heart at this juncture, but the Old Master knew better.

He simply counted declarer's known points: two for the ◇Q and five for the ♠A-J, revealed by the play and the bidding. Declarer could not have the ♣A as well. That would make 11 HCP, far too much for a merely invitational 2♠. Since East was marked with the ♣A, the club king concluded, the Old Master played me at trick 6 and a club to the ace took 4♠ one down.

That worked very well on the actual layout, said the diamond six, but with East showing an even number of diamonds, might that not be bottom from a doubleton? If so, South's hand pattern could have been a 5-3-4-1 pattern and the defence would need to cash one club and one heart at the end.

Certainly the ◇4 was consistent with two or four diamonds, replied the ♣K, but with four diamonds, declarer would be tackling trumps at trick 2, not the diamonds where a ruff might ensue. One has to assume some minimum basis of sensible play from declarer.

I hate to rely on the opposition, said the diamond six. I much prefer to trust partner. Consider this problem:

North dealer : Both vulnerable

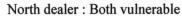

♠ 10 7 5
♡ A Q 9 8 6
◇ Q 9 8 7
♣ 2

♠ A J 8
♡ J 5 3
◇ J 10 5
♣ K J 9 7

WEST	NORTH	EAST	SOUTH	
	Pass	Pass	1♣	West leads the ◇ J: queen
Pass	1♡	Pass	1♠	– king – ace. South returns
Pass	1NT	Pass	2♣	the ◇3: ten – seven – six.
Pass	Pass	Pass		What should West do now?

The power behind the thrown

The story of the ◇6

This was the complete deal:

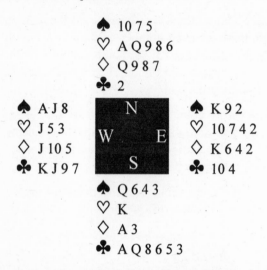

```
                    ♠ 10 7 5
                    ♡ A Q 9 8 6
                    ◇ Q 9 8 7
                    ♣ 2
    ♠ A J 8                         ♠ K 9 2
    ♡ J 5 3          N              ♡ 10 7 4 2
    ◇ J 10 5      W     E           ◇ K 6 4 2
    ♣ K J 9 7        S              ♣ 10 4
                    ♠ Q 6 4 3
                    ♡ K
                    ◇ A 3
                    ♣ A Q 8 6 5 3
```

The bidding strongly suggested that South was 4-6 in the blacks. Why was South so anxious to set up some winners in diamonds? There was no heart loser and so South was aiming to pitch some spades. The Old Master found confirmation for his hypothesis because of me, said the diamond six. I was East's highest diamond and the Old Master read that as a suit-preference signal to show values in spades. With the ♡K instead of the ♠K East would have played the ◇2 under the ◇10, asking for the lower non-trump suit.

It is certainly not attractive to lead from A-J-x into declarer's bid suit, but thanks to me, that is just what the Old Master did. At trick 3 he switched to the ♠8. East won with the ♠K and returned the ♠9. West took two more spades and exited with a heart. The outcome was 2♣ down two.

You can see what would happen if West shifts to a heart after taking the ◇10. Declarer takes the ♡A and pitches a spade on the ♡Q. Next he plays the top diamonds, throwing two more spades. West can ruff the fourth diamond, but only at the expense of a trump trick. Declarer thus loses only one spade, one diamond and three clubs. True, it was only a measly 2♣ contract, but real bridge players take care against contracts at any level.

I know exactly what you mean, said the heart six. Look how East mistreated me on this deal, a modest 2♡ contract:

Two hearts skipped a beat

The story of the ♡6

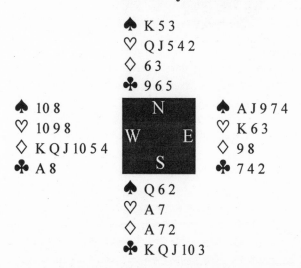

```
              ♠ K 5 3
              ♡ Q J 5 4 2
              ◇ 6 3
              ♣ 9 6 5
♠ 10 8              N              ♠ A J 9 7 4
♡ 10 9 8                          ♡ K 6 3
◇ K Q J 10 5 4  W        E        ◇ 9 8
♣ A 8              S              ♣ 7 4 2
              ♠ Q 6 2
              ♡ A 7
              ◇ A 7 2
              ♣ K Q J 10 3
```

With both sides vulnerable, the Old Master opened 1NT as South in third seat. North bid 2◇, transfer to hearts, and South's 2♡ was passed out. West led the ◇K, taken by the ace. South played the ♣K: eight – five – two. Next came the ♡A: eight – two, and with some misguided idea to show an odd number of trumps, East played me, said the heart six. What a squanderer.

A heart to the queen was won by the king and East returned the ◇8 to West's ten. West was also not paying attention to the spot cards because he continued with the top diamond. He should have known that the only missing spot card in trumps was the three and either shifted to spades or cashed the ♣A and then played a spade.

The Old Master ruffed the ◇Q with the ♡5 and cashed the ♡J, drawing the missing trumps. A club to the queen took out the ace. West now switched to a spade, but the defence took only two spades, a heart, a diamond and a club, when the contract should have been defeated easily.

****

A shudder went through the Old Master's body.

Hold it there, shouted the club ace. I thought I told you earlier we do not want any depressing stories. Surely we can produce deals which have a bright side to them.

I couldn't agree more, said the spade queen. I have a suitable one here. How would you fare as declarer with this problem?

NORTH	North dealer : Nil vulnerable
♠ 9	
♡ A 10 9 3	
◇ A K Q J 10	
♣ Q J 4	

West	North	East	South
	1◇	2♠ (1)	Pass
Pass	Dble	Pass	2NT
Pass	3NT	All pass	

(1) Weak jump-overcall

SOUTH	
♠ Q 3 2	
♡ 5 4 2	
◇ 9 5 3	
♣ A 10 9 7	

West leads the ♠6: nine – king – two and East returns the ♠J.

What would you play as South, the ♠3 or the ♠Q? Make your decision before you look at the complete deal.

Eternal sunshine of the spotless mind

The story of the ♠Q

This was the complete deal:

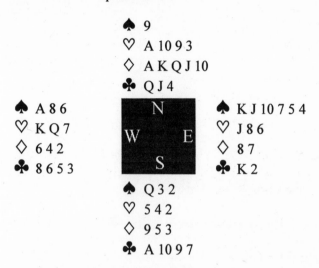

```
                    ♠ 9
                    ♡ A 10 9 3
                    ◇ A K Q J 10
                    ♣ Q J 4
    ♠ A 8 6              N              ♠ K J 10 7 5 4
    ♡ K Q 7                             ♡ J 8 6
    ◇ 6 4 2         W         E         ◇ 8 7
    ♣ 8 6 5 3            S              ♣ K 2
                    ♠ Q 3 2
                    ♡ 5 4 2
                    ◇ 9 5 3
                    ♣ A 10 9 7
```

After ♣6 to the king and the ♠J return, the natural temptation is to rise with the ♠Q, expecting East to have A-K-J-10-x-x. The Old Master resisted the impulse and played low after a brief moment's thought. The defence could take only three tricks and the Old Master finished with an overtrick.

Might it have been right to play you? asked the club two.

Not if the contract was to succeed, replied the spade queen. The Old Master's clear mind instantly saw that if the ♠Q won he would have eight tricks. To make more he needed the ♣K with East, but with ♠A-K-J-10-x-x plus the ♣K East would be too strong for a weak jump-overcall. Placing the ♣K with East as a matter of necessity meant that the ♠A figured to be with West. Hence the Old Master kept me in hand in order to block the spade suit.

And I have another one for you, said the spade queen.

NORTH	East dealer : Nil vulnerable
♠ A Q	
♡ A K Q	West North East South
◇ A 9 8 6 5	Pass 3♣
♣ Q 8 2	Pass 4NT Pass 5◇ (1)
	Pass 6♣ All pass
	(1) One key card for clubs
SOUTH	West leads the ♠J.
♠ 7 5	
♡ 10 5 2	How should South plan the play?
◇ Q 4	Make your decision before you look at
♣ A J 10 9 5 4	the complete deal.

Second-hand story

The next story of the ♠Q

This was the full deal:

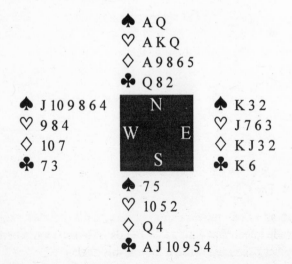

                     ♠ A Q
                     ♡ A K Q
                     ◇ A 9 8 6 5
                     ♣ Q 8 2

♠ J 10 9 8 6 4   ♠ K 3 2
♡ 9 8 4   ♡ J 7 6 3
◇ 10 7   ◇ K J 3 2
♣ 7 3   ♣ K 6

                     ♠ 7 5
                     ♡ 10 5 2
                     ◇ Q 4
                     ♣ A J 10 9 5 4

The club slam is not very good, but who amongst us has not at some time reached a poor slam? The Old Master could see that he had to avoid a club loser and there was an almost certain loser in diamonds. Should he take the spade finesse at trick 1? That would work if West had led from the ♠K and the East had the ♣K.

The Old Master felt West was unlikely to lead from a K-J-10 suit against a slam. In that case finessing me would be futile, said the spade queen. As with my previous deal, he kept me for later. The Old Master and I are clearly close friends.

The Old Master took the ♠A at trick one and led the ♣Q: king – ace – three. The ♣J drew the missing trumps. After the ♡A, ♡K and ♡Q were cashed, these cards remained:

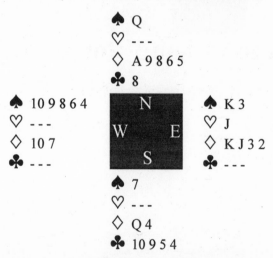

East tried the ♦2. The Old Master played the ♦Q and had his slam.

The Old Master exited with the ♠Q. He hoped that whoever had the ♠K also held the ♦K. So it proved. East won, but had no good move. As a heart or a spade would concede a ruff-and-discard, East tried the ♦2. The Old Master played the ♦Q and had his slam.

That could just as easily have been my story, said the diamond queen, but the spade queen and I are good friends. We have combined successfully on other occasions. Take a look at this deal:

The taming of the shrewd

The story of the ◇Q

East dealer : Both vulnerable

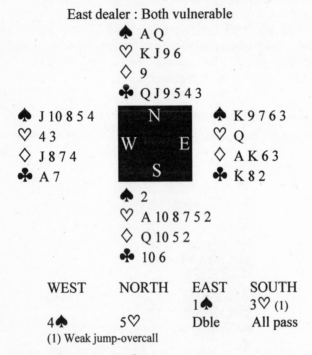

	♠ A Q	
	♡ K J 9 6	
	◇ 9	
	♣ Q J 9 5 4 3	
♠ J 10 8 5 4		♠ K 9 7 6 3
♡ 4 3		♡ Q
◇ J 8 7 4		◇ A K 6 3
♣ A 7		♣ K 8 2
	♠ 2	
	♡ A 10 8 7 5 2	
	◇ Q 10 5 2	
	♣ 10 6	

WEST	NORTH	EAST	SOUTH
		1♠	3♡ (1)
4♠	5♡	Dble	All pass

(1) Weak jump-overcall

West began with the ♣A and in response to East's encouraging signal continued with the ♣7. This was not too wise by either defender, but such is life in the world of bridge. East should have cashed a top diamond at trick 3, but he had a devious plan in mind.

He thought that declarer was certain to have the ♡A and returning the third club would put South to the test. East felt that South would probably rise with the ♡A and then finesse the ♡J. East would thus score the ♡Q for an extra one down. It would not have hurt to cash the ◇A first, but so immersed was East with his little deception that he neglected to take this precaution.

Naturally East had not reckoned with the Old Master, who viewed the third club with suspicion. West was known to have a weak hand for the jump to 4♠. West had already turned up with an ace. Was West likely to have the ♡Q, too? Would West be looking for a ruff if he held ♡Q-x or ♡Q-x-x?

It was possible, but it seemed too unlikely to the Old Master. He ruffed the third club with the ♡5 and West discarded a spade. A heart to the king dropped the bare queen and the ♡J drew the missing trump.

The Old Master cashed dummy's club winners and discarded three diamond losers. He then played two more rounds of trumps ending in his hand. This was the three-card ending:

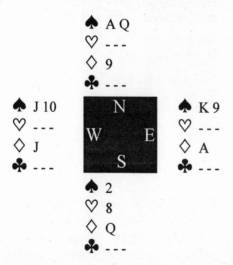

The Old Master played the ♡8 and discarded the ♢9 from dummy. East was finished. He knew that if he threw the ♠9, South would play the ♠2 to the ace. Hoping that I was in the West hand, said the diamond queen, East discarded the ♢A. Thus I had risen to winning rank and 5♡ doubled was made. That is when West leaned across and said to East, "Short of cash, are we?"

You needed an opposition error, said the diamond eight, but I was the essential card to allow the Old Master to succeed on this deal. There was nothing the opponents could do, thanks to me. Not only that, but the end came very early for the defenders.

Trumpled to death

The story of the ◇8

East dealer : Both vulnerable

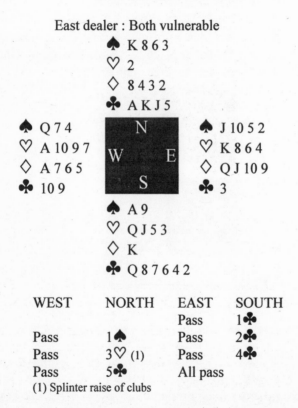

♠ K 8 6 3
♡ 2
◇ 8 4 3 2
♣ A K J 5

♠ Q 7 4
♡ A 10 9 7
◇ A 7 6 5
♣ 10 9

♠ J 10 5 2
♡ K 8 6 4
◇ Q J 10 9
♣ 3

♠ A 9
♡ Q J 5 3
◇ K
♣ Q 8 7 6 4 2

WEST	NORTH	EAST	SOUTH
		Pass	1♣
Pass	1♠	Pass	2♣
Pass	3♡ (1)	Pass	4♣
Pass	5♣	All pass	

(1) Splinter raise of clubs

North's 3♡ showed club support and a singleton or void in hearts. The Old Master toyed with the idea of bidding 3NT, but the poor clubs combined with the singleton diamond deterred him.

West began with the ◇A and promptly switched to the ♣10 when East signalled with the ◇Q and the ◇K dropped from South. The Old Master took the trump shift with dummy's ♣A and played the ♡2. It would do no good for East to rise with the ♡K. East did not have a second trump to lead and to play the ♡K would also expose West to a ruffing finesse in hearts. East played low and the ♡Q lost to the ace.

This was the position at trick 4 with West to lead:

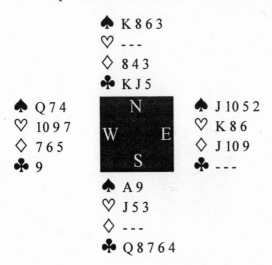

```
            ♠ K 8 6 3
            ♡ - - -
            ◇ 8 4 3
            ♣ K J 5
♠ Q 7 4         N          ♠ J 10 5 2
♡ 10 9 7                   ♡ K 8 6
◇ 7 6 5    W       E       ◇ J 10 9
♣ 9             S          ♣ - - -
            ♠ A 9
            ♡ J 5 3
            ◇ - - -
            ♣ Q 8 7 6 4
```

What was West to do? If he did not play a second trump, declarer would be able to cross-ruff the rest of the hand for eleven tricks. West therefore played the ♣9, but that was just as fatal.

The Old Master won with dummy's ♣K, but East had no good discard. If he threw a spade, ♠A, ♠K and a third spade ruffed would set up dummy's fourth spade. If East ditched a heart, spade to the ace, ♡3 ruffed, diamond ruff, ♡5 ruffed would drop East's king and South's ♡J would be high. Finally, East discarded the ◇9. The Old Master ruffed the ◇3, ruffed a heart and ruffed the ◇4. That made me into a winner, said the diamond eight. Had I been the ◇7 or lower, the contract would have failed.

You were essential, being higher than the ◇7, said the diamond two, but there is no card lower than we twos. When I'm feeling depressed I actually feel lower than the two of clubs, but I have had my moments of triumph. The Old Master used me for a similar purpose to yours on this deal:

Tiny diamond shines through

The story of the ◇2

South dealer : Nil vulnerable

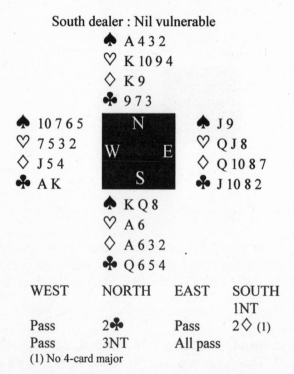

♠ A 4 3 2
♡ K 10 9 4
◇ K 9
♣ 9 7 3

♠ 10 7 6 5   ♠ J 9
♡ 7 5 3 2   ♡ Q J 8
◇ J 5 4   ◇ Q 10 8 7
♣ A K   ♣ J 10 8 2

♠ K Q 8
♡ A 6
◇ A 6 3 2
♣ Q 6 5 4

WEST	NORTH	EAST	SOUTH
			1NT
Pass	2♣	Pass	2◇ (1)
Pass	3NT	All pass	

(1) No 4-card major

Many declarers failed in 3NT, but the Old Master made ten tricks. West led the ♠5: two – jack – king. The Old Master could see seven tricks on top and needed to create two more. The spade lead suggested the spades were not 3-3 and so he tried the ♣4.

This worked well as West won with the ♣K. Fearful that a second spade might help declarer, West switched to the ♢4: nine – queen – three. The ♢7 came back: six – five – king. The Old Master was trying to create an illusion that he had only three diamonds and so he kept me concealed, said the diamond two.

The Old Master continued with the ♣7 from dummy: eight – six – ace and West returned the ♢J: ♡4 – ♢8 – ♢A. The ♠Q was cashed to leave this end-position:

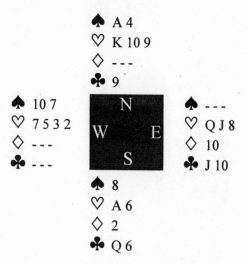

```
              ♠ A 4
              ♡ K 10 9
              ♢ - - -
              ♣ 9
  ♠ 10 7                      ♠ - - -
  ♡ 7 5 3 2      N            ♡ Q J 8
  ♢ - - -    W     E          ♢ 10
  ♣ - - -        S            ♣ J 10
              ♠ 8
              ♡ A 6
              ♢ 2
              ♣ Q 6
```

When the Old Master led the ♠8 to dummy's ace, East was caught in a triple squeeze. A heart discard would give declarer three heart tricks and if East shed the ♣10, that would give South two club tricks. East let go the ♢10, but that made me high, said the diamond two, and merely postponed the inevitable.

After a club to the queen, West throwing a heart, the Old Master cashed me next. This produced a simple squeeze on East, as the cards lay, but if West held one of the heart honours, I would have been the key to a double squeeze. When the Old Master played me, West threw another heart and the ♠4 went from dummy. Whether East threw a club or a heart, South had ten tricks.

You said you sometimes feel lower than me, said the club two, but I never feel low. I always think that I might have a critical part to play. Why I remember when bridge was in its infancy I was the key to preventing Julius Caesar becoming emperor of Rome. It was the result of a challenge match with the crown of Rome at stake.

You brute, Brutus

The story of the ♣2

West dealer : North-South vulnerable

NORTH
♠ K 8 6 4 2
♡ 6
♢ A J 10
♣ 7 6 5 4

SOUTH
♠ A Q J 10 9 7 3
♡ A 8
♢ 7
♣ A K J

WEST	NORTH	EAST	SOUTH
Brutus	*Antony*	*Cassius*	*Caesar*
2NT	Pass	3♣	4♠
Pass	4NT	5♡	5♠
7♡	7♠	All pass	

The Romanus 2NT Convention showed an opening hand with at least 5-5 in the red suits or the black suits. East's 3♣ was 'pass-or-correct'. With South jumping to 4♠ and North using Blackwood, Cassius deduced that West must have the red suits.

West led the ♡K. How would you play in Caesar's position?

On seeing dummy, Caesar boasted, "A fine dummy for a fine declarer. If I fail to make this contract, Antony, it would not be mete for me to wear the crown of Rome. I shall stake my ambition upon the outcome of this deal."

So saying, Caesar won with the ♡A and cashed the ♠A, East following and West discarding the ♡7. The ♣A came next, the ♣9 from West and the ♣3 from East. Caesar ruffed his heart loser and proceeded to run trumps. This was what he saw with one trump to go:

NORTH
♠ - - -
♡ - - -
◇ A J
♣ 7 6

SOUTH
♠ 7
♡ - - -
◇ 7
♣ K J

It was clear from West's opening bid that West's diamonds would be headed by the king-queen. If he also held ♣Q-x-x originally, the last spade would squeeze him. He would have to let go a top diamond or relinquish the guard to the club queen.

On the other hand, if East held the ♣Q a simple finesse would work. Caesar cashed his last trump, discarding a club from dummy. Brutus played the ♣10 (having followed earlier with the ♣9 under the ♣A). The ◇7 came next, king, ace. When dummy's last club was played East followed with the ♣8. East had not discarded any clubs earlier and the moment of truth was at hand. Had the squeeze operated? Should Caesar play the ♣K and drop the bare ♣Q from Brutus or should he finesse cold Cassius for the queen?

Caesar finally decided that the crown of Rome could scarcely be won on a play so mundane as a finesse. Playing the ♣K from his hand, he turned to Brutus:

"Ho, Brutus, what play you on that?"

"A two, Caesar."

"A two?? A two, Brute, then fall Caesar."

The grand slam was one down and I had played a significant role in history, said the club two. This was the full deal:

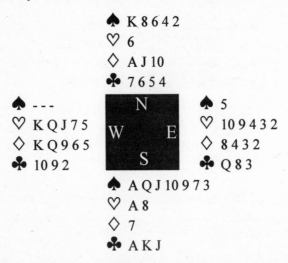

```
              ♠ K 8 6 4 2
              ♡ 6
              ♢ A J 10
              ♣ 7 6 5 4
♠ - - -                        ♠ 5
♡ K Q J 7 5      N            ♡ 10 9 4 3 2
♢ K Q 9 6 5    W   E          ♢ 8 4 3 2
♣ 10 9 2         S            ♣ Q 8 3
              ♠ A Q J 10 9 7 3
              ♡ A 8
              ♢ 7
              ♣ A K J
```

My story is not as amazing as yours, said the heart three, but I was involved in a deal where the bidding convinced the Old Master also to reject a finesse. The auction went like this:

WEST	NORTH	EAST	SOUTH
Pass	1♢	1♡	1♠ (1)
Pass	2♡ (2)	3♡	Pass
Pass	4♠	All pass	

(1) 5+ spades   (2) Strong hand

This was the complete deal:

Leading the charge

The story of the ♡3

West dealer : East-West vulnerable

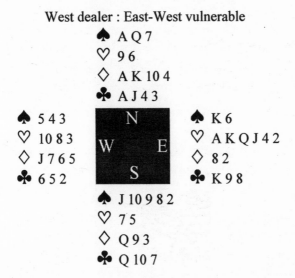

    ♠ A Q 7
    ♡ 9 6
    ◇ A K 10 4
    ♣ A J 4 3

♠ 5 4 3   ♠ K 6
♡ 10 8 3   ♡ A K Q J 4 2
◇ J 7 6 5   ◇ 8 2
♣ 6 5 2   ♣ K 9 8

    ♠ J 10 9 8 2
    ♡ 7 5
    ◇ Q 9 3
    ♣ Q 10 7

West led the ♡8. East won with the queen and cashed the ♡A, on which West followed with the ten (M.U.D.). East was already endplayed and exited with the ◇2 to the jack and king.

East's exuberant bidding at unfavourable vulnerability convinced the Old Master that East held all the significant high cards. He therefore declined the spade finesse and cashed the ♠A at trick 4.

Then came the ◇4 to the queen and a diamond back to dummy's ten. East declined to ruff, but it was irrelevant. The Old Master pitched a club on the ◇A and then played a spade. East won and had the choice of playing a club or conceding a ruff-and-discard. Either way declarer had no club loser and so the Old Master had made his game.

I don't get it, said the diamond four.

What don't you get? asked the heart three.

You said you were involved, yet you played no part whatsoever.

That is precisely the point, said the heart three. I should have been the focal point of the deal. West should be charged for that terrible ♡8 lead. It is wrong to play middle-up-down with 10-x-x. It is standard and should be routine practice to play lowest from three cards headed by any single honour, whether it is from K-x-x or from 10-x-x.

Suppose West had correctly led me, the heart three went on. East can tell West has led his lowest card and that must be either a singleton or bottom from 10-x-x. East can therefore win trick 1 and return the ♡2 at trick 2. West wins (or ruffs) and now a club switch will defeat declarer.

Anyway, I was also involved in a similar situation, the diamond four rejoined. How would you handle this problem?

NORTH	West dealer : Nil vulnerable			
♠ K J	West	North	East	South
♡ 7 5 3 2	1♣	Pass	Pass	Dble
◇ 8 5 2	1♡	Pass	2♣	2♠
♣ 10 9 3 2	Pass	Pass	Pass	
SOUTH	West leads the ♠10.			
♠ A Q 7 5 3				
♡ K 8 4	How should South plan the play?			
◇ A Q J 4				
♣ 8				

The numbers game

The story of the ◇4

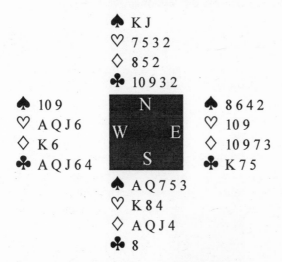

```
              ♠ K J
              ♡ 7 5 3 2
              ◇ 8 5 2
              ♣ 10 9 3 2
♠ 10 9              N              ♠ 8 6 4 2
♡ A Q J 6      W       E          ♡ 10 9
◇ K 6                             ◇ 10 9 7 3
♣ A Q J 6 4        S              ♣ K 7 5
              ♠ A Q 7 5 3
              ♡ K 8 4
              ◇ A Q J 4
              ♣ 8
```

With no attractive lead West began with the ♠10. Your average player might win in dummy and take the diamond finesse at trick 2. That would spell defeat. When the diamonds do not break 3-3 declarer can make only five spades and two diamonds.

The Old Master did not play like that, of course. On the bidding diamonds were unlikely to be 3-3 and the diamond finesse was virtually certain to fail. With clubs headed by the A-K, West would have started with a top club. West's riskier spade lead marked East with the ♣K. Since East passed West's 1♣, East could not have the ◇K as well as the ♣K. Hence the ◇K was with West.

The Old Master took the ♠K, cashed the ♠J, crossed to the ◇A and drew the missing trumps. Then he played me, said the diamond four, and when the ◇K dropped, the Old Master had made his contract.

You low cards take great pleasure in laying the high cards low, said the heart king. Forcing a majestic king to capture only low cards, using us for an endplay, but we can be quite cunning in our own way. Have a look at this deal where I was together with my son, the jack, and the Old Master was playing with his son.

And somewhere hearts are light

The story of the ♡K

North dealer : East-West vulnerable

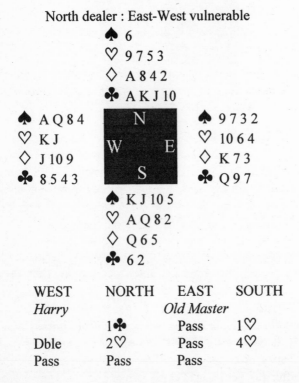

```
              ♠ 6
              ♡ 9 7 5 3
              ◇ A 8 4 2
              ♣ A K J 10
♠ A Q 8 4          N          ♠ 9 7 3 2
♡ K J                         ♡ 10 6 4
◇ J 10 9      W        E      ◇ K 7 3
♣ 8 5 4 3          S          ♣ Q 9 7
              ♠ K J 10 5
              ♡ A Q 8 2
              ◇ Q 6 5
              ♣ 6 2
```

WEST	NORTH	EAST	SOUTH
Harry		*Old Master*	
	1♣	Pass	1♡
Dble	2♡	Pass	4♡
Pass	Pass	Pass	

Harry's double was a bit skimpy, but Harry liked to take chances.

A shudder wracked the Old Master's frame.

Harry led the ◇J, ducked to the king. The Old Master returned the ♡4: two – king! – three. Harry exited with the ♣3. Declarer won with dummy's ace and, playing East for ♡J-10-6-4 originally, continued with the ♡5: six – eight . . . Harry took the ♡J, cashed the ♠A and the contract was one down. The Old Master and Harry, father and son, had combined well to bluff declarer into thinking West had started with me singleton, said the heart king.

****

"Doctor, come quickly."

The Australian coma expert was there at once. Tears were streaming down the Old Master's face. It seemed they would never stop.

"What's going on, doctor?"

"I'm not sure, but something must have triggered a terrible memory. I have never seen anything like this in a coma patient."

****

What did I do? wailed the heart king.

It's your description of how the father and son combined so well and how Harry liked to take chances. You know what happened.

Yes, Harry was killed in a car accident.

It's not just that he died, but how it happened. Harry's friend had borrowed his father's car without permission. He came to the back of Jenny and the Old Master's house and whistled for Harry to come down. Harry climbed out the window and off they went.

Harry's friend had been drinking and he was driving too fast. On a sharp curve he lost control and slammed the car into a pole. They found Harry next day, curled up under the car. His friend had run off after the accident. People drove past, but no one had seen Harry lying there. The police told Jenny and the Old Master that Harry had survived the crash, but died later. If his friend had reported the accident, Harry might have been saved.

I'm terribly sorry, said the heart king. I feel awful.

Maybe I can make up for it, said the spade king. The Old Master used me to good effect, even though I was not in his hand.

To reach the unreachable dummy

The story of the ♠K

West dealer : Both vulnerable

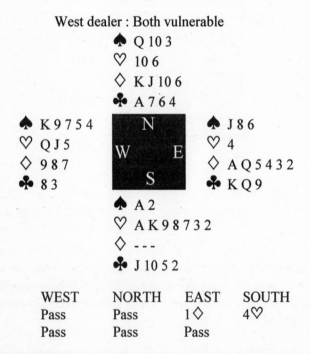

```
                    ♠ Q 10 3
                    ♡ 10 6
                    ◊ K J 10 6
                    ♣ A 7 6 4
  ♠ K 9 7 5 4         N         ♠ J 8 6
  ♡ Q J 5                       ♡ 4
  ◊ 9 8 7         W       E     ◊ A Q 5 4 3 2
  ♣ 8 3               S         ♣ K Q 9
                    ♠ A 2
                    ♡ A K 9 8 7 3 2
                    ◊ - - -
                    ♣ J 10 5 2
```

WEST	NORTH	EAST	SOUTH
Pass	Pass	1◊	4♡
Pass	Pass	Pass	

West began with the ◊8: jack – queen – ruffed. The Old Master cashed the ♡A and ♡K, East discarding the ◊2 as suit-preference for clubs on the second spade. The Old Master continued with a third trump and East threw the ◊3. West dutifully switched to the ♣8, ducked to East's ♣Q and back came the ♠6. Put yourself in the Old Master's position. How would you play on the ♠6 switch?

You can see what would happen if the Old Master had ducked. West would win with me, said the spade king, and play another club. Now South loses two clubs, a heart and a spade.

The Old Master found the winning move. He rose with the ♠A and played a low club to dummy's ace. Then came the ◇K, ace, ruffed by South. This was now the position:

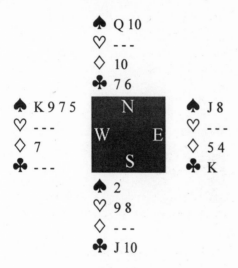

```
                ♠ Q 10
                ♡ - - -
                ◇ 10
                ♣ 7 6
  ♠ K 9 7 5    ┌─────────┐    ♠ J 8
  ♡ - - -      │    N    │    ♡ - - -
  ◇ 7          │  W   E  │    ◇ 5 4
  ♣ - - -      │    S    │    ♣ K
               └─────────┘
                ♠ 2
                ♡ 9 8
                ◇ - - -
                ♣ J 10
```

There was no entry to dummy, but the Old Master used me to get there, said the spade king. In the five-card ending he exited with the ♠2. I took the trick, but I had to give the Old Master access to dummy. I was stepping-stoned. He then ditched his club losers on the ♠Q and the ◇10.

Of course, I could have ducked the ♠2, said the spade king, but it would make no difference. The Old Master could not afford to let East gain the lead and he would have risen with the ♠Q anyway.

I know the repercussions were bad, the diamond jack put a comforting arm around the heart king's shoulder, but I really liked your deal. You might consider what you would do at trick 2 here:

East dealer : Nil vulnerable

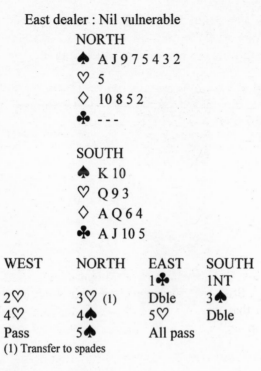

NORTH
♠ A J 9 7 5 4 3 2
♡ 5
◇ 10 8 5 2
♣ - - -

SOUTH
♠ K 10
♡ Q 9 3
◇ A Q 6 4
♣ A J 10 5

WEST	NORTH	EAST	SOUTH
		1♣	1NT
2♡	3♡ (1)	Dble	3♠
4♡	4♠	5♡	Dble
Pass	5♠	All pass	

(1) Transfer to spades

West leads the ♡J. East wins with the king and switches to the ◇J. How should South play?

Switchcraft

The story of the ◇J

What I liked about your deal, the diamond jack was speaking to the heart king, was Harry's deceptive play, winning the first trump trick with the king and not the jack. There is something very appealing about being able to fool declarer and defeating a contract that way. The Old Master used me for that purpose here:

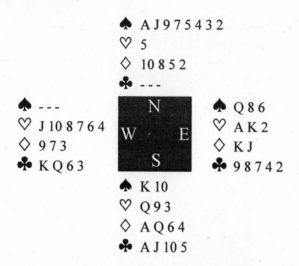

        ♠ A J 9 7 5 4 3 2
        ♡ 5
        ◇ 10 8 5 2
        ♣ - - -

♠ - - -   ♠ Q 8 6
♡ J 10 8 7 6 4   ♡ A K 2
◇ 9 7 3   ◇ K J
♣ K Q 6 3   ♣ 9 8 7 4 2

        ♠ K 10
        ♡ Q 9 3
        ◇ A Q 6 4
        ♣ A J 10 5

Given South's 1NT overcall, North might have passed South's double of 5♡. Still, you can sympathise with North's decision to bid 5♠ with that freakish shape, but 5♡ doubled would be at least two down and one more if South hits on the ♣A lead.

West led the ♡J, won by the king. With barely a moment's thought the Old Master switched to me, said the diamond jack. You can see declarer's dilemma. If the ◇J is a singleton it is fatal to finesse. He rose with the ◇A. This fails only if trumps are 3-0 and so they were. One down, thanks to the Old Master's ingenuity.

If instead East switches to a club at trick 2, declarer is virtually forced to succeed. Win the club trick, play ♠K and ♠A, followed by a low diamond. With the really lucky diamond layout, South loses only one heart and one spade.

I fully agree with you, said the spade ten. Larceny is lovely. Deception is delicious. I have a story in similar vein. The Old Master used me for a psychic bid and subsequently scored a trick with me even though I was a singleton and the opponents could have captured the trick in the suit. Here is the deal . . .

Trick question

The story of the ♠10

East dealer : Both vulnerable

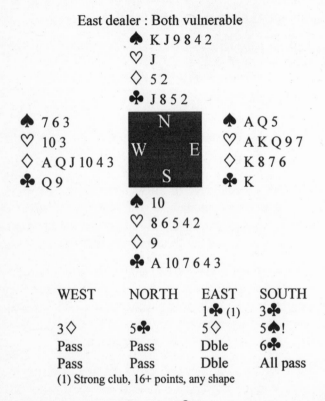

```
                    ♠ K J 9 8 4 2
                    ♡ J
                    ◇ 5 2
                    ♣ J 8 5 2
♠ 7 6 3                                ♠ A Q 5
♡ 10 3              N                  ♡ A K Q 9 7
◇ A Q J 10 4 3    W   E                ◇ K 8 7 6
♣ Q 9              S                   ♣ K
                    ♠ 10
                    ♡ 8 6 5 4 2
                    ◇ 9
                    ♣ A 10 7 6 4 3
```

WEST	NORTH	EAST	SOUTH
		1♣ (1)	3♣
3◇	5♣	5◇	5♠!
Pass	Pass	Dble	6♣
Pass	Pass	Dble	All pass

(1) Strong club, 16+ points, any shape

The Old Master's jump to 3♣ looks dangerous, but hands with freak shape make more tricks than their strength suggests. When North made a shapely raise to 5♣ (4◇ would show a strong raise to 5♣) the Old Master wanted to buy the contract and not have the opponents bid 6◇, which happens to be unbeatable. He decided to make a fake lead-directing bid of 5♠. East naturally assumed that this was showing a void and so settled for doubling South. It would look silly to bid 6◇ and go down on a spade ruff.

The defence began with the ♡10 lead, followed by two rounds of diamonds. The Old Master ruffed, cashed the ♣A, ruffed a heart in dummy and led a low spade. East was not about to have his ♠Q ruffed and so he played low. Thus I won the trick, said the spade ten, and the Old Master was only two down, a great result as his team-mates bid and made 6♢ in the other room.

That was excellent, laughed the diamond ten. You might like to consider this problem, which arose in a game of rubber bridge:

South dealer : Both vulnerable

NORTH

♠ K J 9 8 5

♡ 10 6

♢ Q 10 7 3

♣ A 10

SOUTH

♠ Q

♡ A K Q 7 5 3

♢ K 8 6 2

♣ 7 6

WEST	NORTH	EAST	SOUTH
	Old Master		*Jenny*
			1♡
Pass	1♠	Pass	2♡
Pass	Pass	2NT (1)	Dble
3♣	4♡	All pass	

(1) Takeout for the minors

After Jenny doubled 2NT the Old Master figured she would have extra values and so he made an imaginative jump to 4♡.

West led the ♢9. How would you plan the play as declarer?

A tricky trick

The story of the ◇10

This was the full deal:

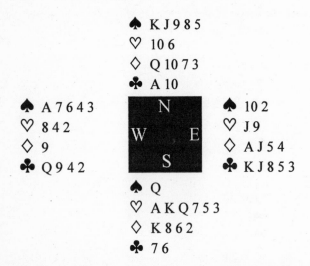

```
                    ♠ K J 9 8 5
                    ♡ 10 6
                    ◇ Q 10 7 3
                    ♣ A 10
♠ A 7 6 4 3              N              ♠ 10 2
♡ 8 4 2         W           E          ♡ J 9
◇ 9                     S              ◇ A J 5 4
♣ Q 9 4 2                              ♣ K J 8 5 3
                    ♠ Q
                    ♡ A K Q 7 5 3
                    ◇ K 8 6 2
                    ♣ 7 6
```

As soon as dummy appeared Jenny realised that West's ◇9 lead was a singleton. She could afford to lose two diamonds, but not if a club switch came before the ♠A was dislodged. If she played me from dummy, said the diamond ten, East might take the ◇A and return the ◇4. West would ruff and shift to a club.

I was actually the key to the deal, said the diamond ten, because Jenny did *not* play me. That lured East into playing low and Jenny won with the ◇K. She drew trumps and played the ♠Q. West won, but the defence could collect only one spade and two diamonds. Making 4♡.

The Old Master beamed, got up from his chair and came over to give Jenny a congratulatory peck on the cheek.

Here is another deal where I was involved, said the diamond ten. You might like to look at it first as a play problem:

North dealer : East-West vulnerable

♠ A 7 6 4
♡ K 2
◇ 10 8 3
♣ 7 6 5 4

SOUTH
♠ Q 9
♡ A Q 6 4
◇ A K 6 5 2
♣ K J

WEST	NORTH	EAST	SOUTH
	Pass	Pass	1◇
Pass	1♠	Pass	2NT
Pass	3NT	All pass	

West leads the ♣2, fourth-highest, to East's ♣Q. It looks as though the clubs are 4-3. How would you plan the play?

Clearly the diamonds have to be developed and there will be no trouble if they are 3-2. South loses one diamond and presumably just three clubs. But what if the diamonds are 4-1? Can you deal with that situation?

Pinpoint accuracy

The second story of the ◇10

This was the complete deal:

```
              ♠ A 7 6 4
              ♡ K 2
              ◇ 10 8 3
              ♣ 7 6 5 4
♠ K J 10 8         N          ♠ 5 3 2
♡ 9 8 5 3                     ♡ J 10 7
◇ 9           W       E       ◇ Q J 7 4
♣ A 10 8 2         S          ♣ Q 9 3
              ♠ Q 9
              ♡ A Q 6 4
              ◇ A K 6 5 2
              ♣ K J
```

Against 3NT West led the ♣2: four – queen – king. If diamonds were 4-1 and East had a singleton honour, cashing a top diamond followed by a low diamond would limit the diamond losers to one. That would not work if West had the singleton.

West was slightly more likely to have the singleton, but there was another advantage to playing West to be short in diamonds. If West had a singleton queen or jack, there would always be two diamond losers if the defence did not slip. However, the defence might slip and if West had started with the singleton nine or seven, then East could be held to one diamond trick.

You can see what would happen if declarer plays a top diamond next. East will then win two diamond tricks and 3NT is one off.

At trick 2 the Old Master played the ♡4 to the king and followed up with me, said the diamond ten. This might tempt East to cover with J-9-7-4 or Q-9-7-4. Alternatively I could pin West's singleton ◇9 or ◇7 if East had Q-J-7-4 or Q-J-9-4. In any of these cases declarer can hold the diamond losers to one, but only if South starts with me.

In practice East covered the ◇10 with the ◇Q, taken by the ace and West's ◇9 dropped. The Old Master continued with the ◇2 to dummy's ◇8. East won and returned a club. West won three club tricks, but the Old Master could later finesse in diamonds for nine tricks.

It makes you feel so important when you are the vital card on a deal, said the club four. I had a special role to play when the Old Master was faced with this problem:

East dealer : Both vulnerable

     ♠ Q 8 6 4 3
     ♡ A K J
     ◇ A 2
     ♣ A 6 2

SOUTH
♠ 5
♡ 5 4 3
◇ K 3
♣ K Q J 10 9 8 4

WEST	NORTH	EAST	SOUTH
		Pass	3♣
Pass	6♣	All pass	

West leads the ♡10. How would you plan the play? If you win with the ace or king, East plays the ♡2, low-like. How would you continue from there?

Lady and the trump

The story of the ♣4

The deal looked like this:

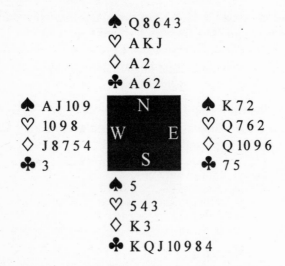

```
                    ♠ Q 8 6 4 3
                    ♡ A K J
                    ◇ A 2
                    ♣ A 6 2
    ♠ A J 10 9          N          ♠ K 7 2
    ♡ 10 9 8                        ♡ Q 7 6 2
    ◇ J 8 7 5 4      W     E        ◇ Q 10 9 6
    ♣ 3                 S           ♣ 7 5
                    ♠ 5
                    ♡ 5 4 3
                    ◇ K 3
                    ♣ K Q J 10 9 8 4
```

Knowing that the Old Master's 3♣ opening vulnerable was expected to have seven tricks, North had four winners to bring the tally to eleven tricks. There was potential for an extra trick in hearts, possibly a ruff in diamonds and maybe the spades would be useful. Bidding 6♣ entailed risk, but then, that is what bridge is all about: Do you have the courage to take the risks?

West led the ♡10: king – two (low encourage) – three. The Old Master immediately played a low spade: two – five – nine. West returned the ♡9, taken by the ace and a low spade was ruffed with the ♣K. The Old Master continued with the ♣Q and then the ♣J to dummy's ♣A. A third spade was ruffed, this time with the ♣8. Have you noticed how the Old Master was keeping me intact? said the ♣4. This was now the position:

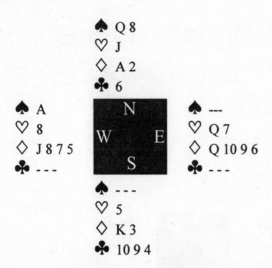

The ◇3 went to the ace and the ♠8 was ruffed with the ♣9 and that set up the spade lady. Now my turn came, said the club four. Had I been played any sooner or used for ruffing declarer would not be able to reach dummy. I was the access key. The ♣6 won and the ♠Q allowed the Old Master to pitch the losing heart.

It warms my heart, said the club three, when we low cards can play such a critical role. I have also been vital from time to time, but before you hear my story, take a look at this lead problem:

North dealer : Both vulnerable				What should West lead from:
WEST	NORTH	EAST	SOUTH	
	2♡ (1)	Pass	4♣ (2)	♠ 8 7 5 3
Pass	5♣	Pass	Pass	♡ A Q 6
Dble	Pass	Pass	Pass	◇ Q 5 3
(1) 7-10 points, 5 hearts and a 4+ minor				♣ A Q 3
(2) Pass-or-correct, strong in both minors				

The little trump

The story of the ♣3

This was the actual deal:

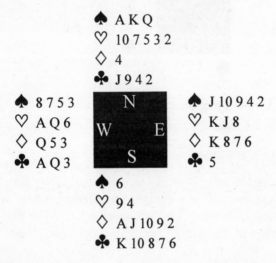

             ♠ A K Q
             ♡ 10 7 5 3 2
             ♢ 4
             ♣ J 9 4 2

♠ 8 7 5 3   ♠ J 10 9 4 2
♡ A Q 6   ♡ K J 8
♢ Q 5 3   ♢ K 8 7 6
♣ A Q 3   ♣ 5

             ♠ 6
             ♡ 9 4
             ♢ A J 10 9 2
             ♣ K 10 8 7 6

As South had length in both minors, North figured South would be short in hearts and so he pushed on to 5♣ and the Old Master doubled. Had he started with a top heart, that would have led to an easy two down, but even the Old Master is not as omniscient as Deep Finesse. The ♣A would also have worked well, since a heart switch would be obvious at trick 2, but the Old Master opted for a passive spade lead.

Declarer quickly played the top spades and ditched his heart losers. He then embarked on a crossruff: ♢A, diamond ruff, heart ruff, diamond ruff, heart ruff to reach this position:

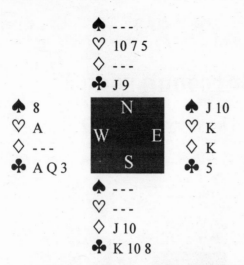

When declarer played the ◇J, the Old Master discarded the ♡A – that was essential – and dummy ruffed. Dummy's next heart was ruffed with the ♣8, over-ruffed, and we were down to three cards:

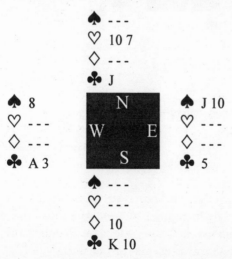

The Old Master cashed the ♣A and played the ♠8. South ruffed and I won trick 13, said the club three. I was the top trump after only one round of trumps had been played.

Bravo, said the heart queen. That was a very satisfying experience. I have had quite a few, too, but this one was special for me:

Surround sound

The story of the ♡Q

East dealer : Both vulnerable

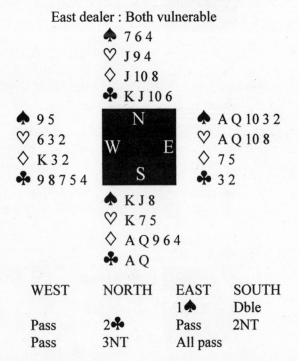

```
                    ♠ 7 6 4
                    ♡ J 9 4
                    ◇ J 10 8
                    ♣ K J 10 6

♠ 9 5                   N                   ♠ A Q 10 3 2
♡ 6 3 2          W           E              ♡ A Q 10 8
◇ K 3 2                                     ◇ 7 5
♣ 9 8 7 5 4             S                   ♣ 3 2

                    ♠ K J 8
                    ♡ K 7 5
                    ◇ A Q 9 6 4
                    ♣ A Q
```

WEST	NORTH	EAST	SOUTH
		1♠	Dble
Pass	2♣	Pass	2NT
Pass	3NT	All pass	

West led the ♠9 and the Old Master won with the ace. He paused for just a moment. His thoughts had gone to Jenny. She was the queen of his heart and so he played me, said the queen of hearts. Declarer covered with the king, played the ♣A, followed by the ♣Q. He overtook with the ♣K and led the ◇J: five – four – king. West returned a heart and the Old Master collected three heart tricks to take the contract one down.

For me this deal epitomised the Old Master's life. Jenny was the one and only for him and I was the one and only card at trick 2 to beat the contract. Jenny surrounded her family with love and I was needed to surround dummy's jack to beat the contract.

"Why are you doing this?" A loud, strange voice boomed across the cards. The spirit of the Old Master had entered their domain. "Why can't you leave me alone? I want to join Jenny. I want to join my son and my daughter. I want to die."

I don't think you do, said the heart queen. If you really wanted to die, you would have done so by now. You could have given up completely and let yourself go. Why has that not happened? Something is tugging at you to remain. What might that be?

"I cannot imagine."

Love is holding you back, said the heart queen.

"You don't know what you are talking about. All my loved ones have gone."

Not all. I can see it in the way you play your cards. The evidence is clear. This is a typical example . . . I'm sure you will recall the deal. It happened in the New Year Teams . . .

Love is the key

The story of the ♠2

East dealer : Both vulnerable

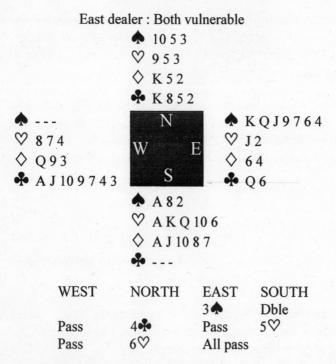

♠ 10 5 3
♡ 9 5 3
◇ K 5 2
♣ K 8 5 2

♠ - - -
♡ 8 7 4
◇ Q 9 3
♣ A J 10 9 7 4 3

♠ K Q J 9 7 6 4
♡ J 2
◇ 6 4
♣ Q 6

♠ A 8 2
♡ A K Q 10 6
◇ A J 10 8 7
♣ - - -

WEST	NORTH	EAST	SOUTH
		3♠	Dble
Pass	4♣	Pass	5♡
Pass	6♡	All pass	

West might have chosen the ♣A for the opening lead, but that would have been fatal for the defence. He opted for a trump instead and you captured East's jack with the ace. You drew a second round of trumps with the ♡K and then led the ◇J: three – two – four. A diamond to the king and a diamond to the ace cleared up the diamonds and revealed the trump position. You continued the diamonds and West had a problem. If he ruffed you would discard a spade from dummy. West would be endplayed and have to give you a club trick. West discarded two clubs on your last two diamonds as you discarded two spades. That left this ending:

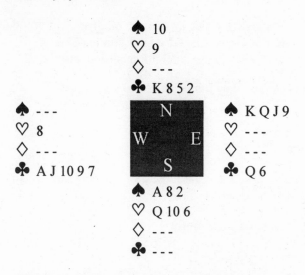

The spirit of the Old Master nodded.

You could have continued with the ♠A, said the heart queen. If West ruffs, he has to give you the ♣K for one spade discard and your other spade loser is ruffed. But what did you do?

I exited with the two of spades.

Exactly, said the heart queen. The result was exactly the same. East won and played a club, ruffed. You finished off the play by ruffing the ♠8, ruffing another club and finally drawing the last trump before taking your ace of spades.

I think I see what you mean ...

You did not use me, said the heart queen, on the first two rounds of trumps. You like to keep me as long as you can. Why? Because of love. Because I remind you of Jenny. You like to use your lowest cards, such as the ♠2 here, whenever you can. Why? Because of love. You have always loved your little ones. That is why you have been torn between the desire to die and the desire to cling on. It is time for you to return.

The Old Master blinked. He slowly opened his eyes. He could see nurses. He saw the coma specialist and another doctor. He saw his son-in-law and his three grandchildren sitting quietly.

As his eyes stayed open, they jumped and shouted,

"Grandpa!"

"Look. He's awake!"

"What happened?" asked the Old Master. "Where am I? In hospital? Where have I been? Am I back?"

The coma specialist answered briefly:

"Check, mate."

Appendix 1

Prequel

The Old Master

The early days

Last Board

© Bridge World Magazine Inc. 1971

The Bridgerama commentator's voice boomed across the audience. *Bermuda Bowl as good as over ... three boards left ... Challengers 33 imps down ... even the Old Master's magic can't help now.*

The Old Master looked down at his cards, though their pasteboard patterns were indelibly etched in his mind. Three boards. He glanced across at his partner. Zettner's brow was furrowed too. Despite some good pickups in this last session, they must still be at least 30 or more imps down. The champions, Frawley-Kinston, were silent – they knew the title was theirs once again. Five years they had held the world crown, and the sixth was merely minutes away. 56 imps up – 16 boards to play. No team in the Bowl could recover that ground. Even counting some sure losses, they had to be well ahead.

As the Old Master waited for the next hand, the old question rose once more. Could this be the one, the perfect hand, the work of art? What was the perfect hand? Was Culbertson right? Was it nothing more than success stemming from opponents' errors? What was beauty in bridge anyway? Was it nine top tricks in 3NT? Though he couldn't pin it down, he felt that there had to be something more, some intangible combination of power in the cards.

Suddenly, he felt very tired, recalling the dilemma in which he constantly found himself in his 40 years' playing. Percentages or elegance? Play to win or play for perfection? Before him rose the shades of games and tournaments lost because he could never quite resolve which he wanted. He remembered the hand that had cost him the Olympiad because he played for the squeeze rather than the finesse.

Frawley's pass woke him from his reverie. The dream of the perfect hand faded. His partner opened 1♢ and Kinston interposed 2♡, a weak bid based on long hearts. The Old Master looked at his hand:

> ♠ J 7 6 4
> ♡ - - -
> ♢ 9
> ♣ A K Q J 9 7 6 4

A straightforward 3♣? 4♣ to emphasize their solidity? The scientists would know – they would get to the cold grand slam or avoid the unmakeable small slam, but their tortuous approach repelled him – too often it pointed the way to astute defenders. Neither side was vulnerable.

"Six clubs."

He smiled wryly, imagining what the commentators would be saying. A leap into the unknown. It could be disastrous, but it was no time to be dainty. The likely heart lead might give him time to work on the diamonds.

Frawley looked up quickly, paused slightly and passed. Zettner passed and Kinston doubled. Lightner. A diamond lead. A bad sign. All passed, and the ♢2 was led.

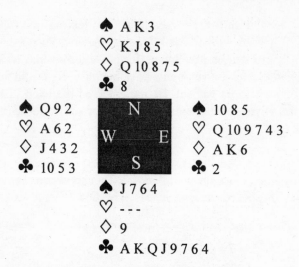

```
                        ♠ A K 3
                        ♡ K J 8 5
                        ◇ Q 10 8 7 5
                        ♣ 8
        ♠ Q 9 2                         ♠ 10 8 5
        ♡ A 6 2                         ♡ Q 10 9 7 4 3
        ◇ J 4 3 2                       ◇ A K 6
        ♣ 10 5 3                        ♣ 2
                        ♠ J 7 6 4
                        ♡ - - -
                        ◇ 9
                        ♣ A K Q J 9 7 6 4
```

The Old Master called for a low diamond and the ◇K won.

In the Closed Room, North-South reached 3NT and made ten tricks, the commentator told the audience. *If 6♣ is made, the challengers will gain 12 imps, but unless East makes the fatal ◇A continuation, South will have to lose a spade ultimately. I predict East will exit with the ♣2.*

East thought for some time, then the trump appeared. The Old Master won and drew two more rounds of trumps, discarding two hearts from dummy. East discarded the seven and four of hearts. The Old Master stopped to think. East began with the ace-king of diamonds. Not the ace of hearts – that would be too strong for a weak jump-overcall. Six hearts headed by the queen. Kinston was strict about suit quality. With seven he would have bid 3♡, without the queen the suit would have been too poor.

Probably he was 3-6-3-1 with 9 points. That must be all, for the queen of spades would also make the hand too strong for a 'weak' two hearts. So, West held the ♠Q, ♡A and the ◇J. That might be just too much to manage.

Suddenly, the Old Master was no longer tired. As he pieced the play together, conviction refreshed him. He played three more rounds of clubs, pitching a spade, a diamond, and the ♡J. West threw a diamond and two hearts; East discarded hearts. This was the position:

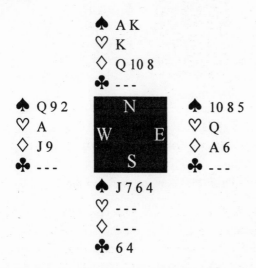

The Old Master played another club and watched West writhe. If West discarded a spade the ace-king would drop the queen, while a diamond discard would allow the jack to be pinned. West studied for a long time and finally ditched the ♡A, but the hand was an open book. A spade to dummy, followed by the ♡K put West in the vice again. He threw the ◇9; the Old Master reached across and touched the ◇Q, murmuring softly, "The pin is mightier than the sword." As East covered and West dropped the jack, the hand was over.

A triple squeeze . . . brilliancy ... Old Master still has spark of genius . . . 10 years since he played internationally . . . included in Challengers' team as sentimental gesture . . . long career . . . now proved back to his best . . . assured of second in world . . . 12 imps to Challengers . . . not enough to stave off defeat . . .

In the Open Room, Frawley growled at Kinston, "A spade return at trick two beats it. Takes out his entry prematurely."

"Sure. And I also knew South didn't have jack-nine-fourth in spades, didn't I?"

The Old Master looked at them sorrowfully. Why was there always so much rancour at the top? He looked as Frawley sat, tight-lipped, stubborn – Frawley, contemptuous of opponents and partners alike – acknowledged as the world's best, yet unable to brook losing a game or a match.

These thoughts were brushed aside as the Old Master picked up the cards. Second-last hand. At least they had made a fight of it. They were vulnerable against not. His partner, dealer, passed. So did Kinston. The Old Master looked at:

$$\spadesuit \ \text{A}$$
$$\heartsuit \ \text{A K 6 2}$$
$$\diamondsuit \ \text{K J 10 9 2}$$
$$\clubsuit \ \text{K 4 3}$$

and opened 1 $\diamondsuit$. Frawley cleared his throat. "Three spades." Pass from Zettner, pass from Kinston, what now?

"Four hearts."

"Four spades."

The Old Master looked at Frawley curiously. A bead of perspiration rested on Frawley's brow. Was he shaken, that fine bridge mind, the leading theorist in the world? Frawley, who had expounded 'pre-empt what you are worth', breaking his own tenets? Three spades, then four spades. Why not four spades at once? The Old Master noticed a slight tremble in Frawley's left hand.

Zettner, patting his hair nervously, tugging at a loose strand, pondered, then bid 5♡. Kinston's double was loud and crisp, and everyone passed. Frawley pulled out the ♠K, and dummy came down.

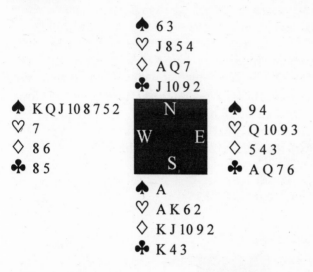

<pre>
                      ♠ 6 3
                      ♡ J 8 5 4
                      ◇ A Q 7
                      ♣ J 10 9 2

♠ K Q J 10 8 7 5 2   N   ♠ 9 4
♡ 7   W   E   ♡ Q 10 9 3
◇ 8 6   S   ◇ 5 4 3
♣ 8 5   ♣ A Q 7 6

                      ♠ A
                      ♡ A K 6 2
                      ◇ K J 10 9 2
                      ♣ K 4 3
</pre>

Closed Room . . . four spades doubled . . . two down . . . plus 300 to Champions . . . headed for big swing . . . South must lose two hearts and a club at least . . . five diamonds a chance . . . five hearts hopeless . . . bad split . . .

The Old Master surveyed the two hands. East would obviously have four trumps at least, maybe five. Prospects were not good. Winning with the ♠A, he played the ◇J. Frawley played the ◇8 as a matter of doubleton reflex, then pulled his hand away as if burnt. The Old Master suddenly saw a glimmer of hope as dummy's ◇7 became a third entry. Could West have a key singleton in trumps?

Dummy's ◇A won and the ♡J was played. The Old Master felt his heart pounding . . . was there a chance after all?

If East held Q-10-9-7 of hearts, all was lost. The ♡Q topped the ♡J, the Old Master played his ace and looked at Frawley's card. It was the ♡7.

The first hurdle was over. Would the other cards behave also? The Old Master moved into the strange world of bridge intuition. Lines of play ran through his mind, the cards swirled into patterns, disappeared, regrouped, blended into a position six tricks away. The Old Master, satisfied with his plan, played the ♢10 to the ♢Q and called for dummy's ♣J. Kinston played low. So did the others. Another club from dummy. This time Kinston took his ♣A and forced South with a spade return. The Old Master ruffed with the ♡2 and reviewed the situation.

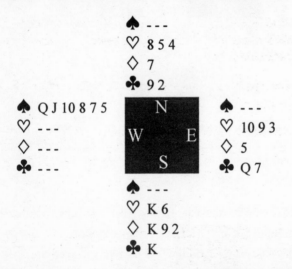

```
                    ♠  - - -
                    ♡  8 5 4
                    ♢  7
                    ♣  9 2
  ♠ Q J 10 8 7 5      N        ♠  - - -
  ♡  - - -                     ♡  10 9 3
  ♢  - - -        W       E    ♢  5
  ♣  - - -                     ♣  Q 7
                      S
                    ♠  - - -
                    ♡  K 6
                    ♢  K 9 2
                    ♣  K
```

No, there was no flaw. It had to be right. He played the ♣K and crossed to dummy's ♢7 with his well-preserved ♢2. The Old Master carefully picked over the end position he had seen before. There was no escape. A low trump was played from dummy. East sat there thinking. He would have to split the ten-nine, thought the Old Master; if not, I win with the ♡6, cash the ♡K, and play a diamond, discarding my losing club from dummy.

Kinston thought interminably; finally, the ♡9. Declarer played the
♡K, and then, luxuriously, treasuring the touch, the Old Master played
a diamond and put the ♡8 on from dummy.

Brilliant timing and end play, the Rama commentator shrieked
shrilly. If East overruffs and plays a club, South ruffs in hand and
ruffs the last diamond in dummy. If East overruffs and plays a
trump, South wins and his hand is high. And if East discards his club,
dummy's club promotes South's six of trumps . . .

The Old Master wondered what was happening. Had the
commentators seen the position as he had? Was there any chance of
snatching victory from the jaws of defeat? The last two hands had to be
gains, but how close was the fight? He could not hear the commentator.

. . . Plus 850 to Challengers . . . 11 imps . . . exciting finish . . .
Champions still 10 imps up . . . additional drama . . . youth versus
age . . . fantastic finale . . .

The audience hushed as the lights on the Bridgerama board
flickered, then lit up the last hand.

Dealer East : East-West vulnerable

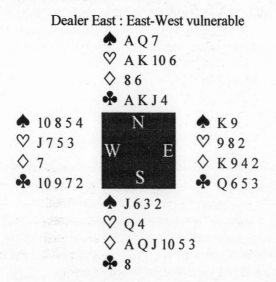

	♠ A Q 7	
	♡ A K 10 6	
	◇ 8 6	
	♣ A K J 4	
♠ 10 8 5 4	N	♠ K 9
♡ J 7 5 3	W E	♡ 9 8 2
◇ 7	S	◇ K 9 4 2
♣ 10 9 7 2		♣ Q 6 5 3
	♠ J 6 3 2	
	♡ Q 4	
	◇ A Q J 10 5 3	
	♣ 8	

The commentator broke into an excited jabber, *Closed Room . . .*
Champions overboard . . . reached 7NT . . . trying to duplicate
probable gamble in Open Room . . . two down . . . Challengers
have chance . . . must stay out of slam . . . game gives them 11
imps and victory . . . slam doomed . . . bad diamond break . . . spade
finesse loses . . .

In the Open Room, the silence was almost unbearable. The Old
Master knew what the others were thinking. Last board. How small
was the margin? Was there a chance or was the match already
over? The audience already knew, but the players had to gauge the
results for themselves. He looked at his hand:

> ♠ J 6 3 2
> ♡ Q 4
> ♢ A Q J 10 5 3
> ♣ 8

Six diamonds and four spades. The opponents were vulnerable,
they were not. He was second to speak. The age-old question
arose, to pre-empt or not to pre-empt? The 'authorities' said not to
pre-empt with a side four-card major, also that a pre-empt by
second hand was less desirable, as one opponent had already passed.
He made up *his* mind. The thought of the perfect hand casually
flitted through him. He dismissed it as Kinston passed quickly.

"Three diamonds."

Pass from Frawley, nervously. Zettner sat for an eternity. The
Old Master knew he must be thinking about slam chances, and
was pleased his diamond suit was respectable. Pre-empts at
favourable vulnerability can often be filthy.

As the minutes toiled on, the audience became restless.

3NT . . . why doesn't he bid 3NT? . . . how can he think of a slam
with nothing in diamonds? . . . 5 ♢ is all right too . . .

"Six diamonds."

The audience groaned.

Three passes followed quickly. Frawley sat for some time considering his lead, then the ♣10 hit the table. The Old Master surveyed the dummy and his own hand.

♠ A Q 7
♡ A K 10 6
◇ 8 6
♣ A K J 4

♠ J 6 3 2
♡ Q 4
◇ A Q J 10 5 3
♣ 8

The slam was reasonable. Had they reached it in the other room? If he didn't lose a diamond trick, the slam was home. With a diamond loser, he still had chances – the ♡J might fall in three rounds, the spade finesse was there, and the ♣Q might appear. He looked at the lead. The ♣10. Had Frawley led away from the ♣Q? Would the club finesse work at trick one? Not a tempting lead against a small slam.

The Old Master played the ♣K and took the diamond finesse. The ◇Q held. He played the ♡4 to the ♡K and another diamond to the ◇J. Frawley showed out.

. . . *If he makes the slam, Challengers win by 4 imps . . . if he goes down, Champions have lucky escape . . .*

The Old Master searched his mind. It was merely a matter of taking all the chances in the right order. One of them would probably succeed. But the quest for perfection tortured him. Painfully, he scanned dummy again. Once more he searched the position, wondering why he was hesitating, why he did not continue.

Suddenly he saw it, and everything else faded except the cards as they glided into their predestined place. Again the testing of each play, racked by the error of his original analysis, soothed by what he could see unfolding before him. Finally, he played the ♢A, discarding the low spade from dummy, then the ♡Q, dropping dummy's ♡6 on it.

♠ A Q
♡ A 10
♢ - - -
♣ A J 4

♠ J 6 3 2
♡ - - -
♢ 10 5 3
♣ - - -

The Old Master considered the final position cherishingly. The aces . . . the master cards . . . one in each suit in dummy . . . each supported by a different lower honour, side by side . . . each tenace agape waiting for East to yield up the twelfth trick . . . each suit having a finesse available in it . . . but the only finesse taken successfully turning out not to gain a trick . . . the suits blending together, in harmony and unison, to succeed no matter where the enemy cards lay.

The victory was his. He had but to take it. With trembling fingers he took the ◇ 10, putting East on lead, softly asked for dummy's ♣4, and whispered gently to the opposition a single word.

"Checkmate."

[*Last Board* was freely based on *Last Round*, a brilliant chess story by Kester Svendsen. *Last Board* first appeared in *The Bridge World* in December, 1971. Subscriptions to *The Bridge World* are available from the www.bridgeworld.com website.]

Last Round

© Bridge World Magazine Inc. 1986 (August issue)

"*. . . World Pairs as good as over . . .*" *boomed the voice of the Bridgerama commentator.* "*320 pairs originally . . . 96 in the semi-finals . . . last of the arduous twenty rounds to find the world's best . . . leaders began final session with three tops advantage . . . now extended to almost seven tops with eight boards to play . . . insurmountable lead . . . even the Old Master's magic can't help now . . .*"

The Old Master entered the sealed room and sat down. They had started the session three boards behind, but well clear of third place. The session had been sound, but not spectacular. Had they made any inroads on the leaders? He glanced at the champions, Frawley and Kinston. They looked confident, self-satisfied – they knew the title was theirs once again.

The Old Master glanced across at his partner, Zettner, who seemed worn out after almost ten days. The Old Master gave him a reassuring nod as he pulled out the cards for Board 17:

Dealer North : Nil vulnerable

♠ K Q 7 6 4
♡ K 9
♢ Q J 4
♣ J 5 2

♠ J 10 9 8
♡ 10 8 7 4
♢ 8 5
♣ 7 6 3

♠ 5 3 2
♡ J 5 2
♢ 10 9 7 3 2
♣ Q 10

♠ A
♡ A Q 6 3
♢ A K 6
♣ A K 9 8 4

"Results from the other tables are in . . . twelve tables made the overtrick in 6NT, two pairs made 7♣ and one made 7NT . . . very lucky club position."

The red light flashed, informing the players that the audience was ready. As the players bid their hands, the monitor relayed the information to the audience. "One spade by North. Three clubs from South. North, four clubs; South four no-trumps; North, five clubs; South, five no-trumps; North, six hearts. Seven no-trumps by South – all pass."

"When you're hot, you're hot . . . shared top for the Champs . . . further ahead after this board . . ."

Zettner led the jack of spades. Kinston put down the dummy. The Old Master sitting East surveyed the dummy. Not much there for an opening bid. Frawley must have the unseen high cards, including the top clubs. No chance to beat the slam, or was there? A glimmer of hope flitted through the Old Master's mind as Frawley won with the spade ace, and continued with the ace of clubs: three, two, *queen*.

With a grin Frawley made the most of his luck . . . nine of clubs, six, five . . . the faintest fraction of a pause and then the ten of clubs claimed the trick.

"Brilliant deception . . . converted bottom into a top . . . not enough to change the outcome."

There was stony silence in the room. It reminded the Old Master of the scene between Frawley and himself eleven years earlier, not long after he and Zettner had wrested the Bowl from the Champions with a whirlwind finish. Frawley had vowed vengeance, and had taken it. The Old Master flushed at the bitter memory. The flashing light brought him back to the present, and he started on Board 18. The bidding began with a 1♡ opening by the Old Master. Then it continued:

WEST	NORTH	EAST	SOUTH
		1♡	Pass
2♣	Double	2◇	Pass
?			

Zettner, West, was looking at:

♠ Q 10 5 3
♡ J 4 2
◇ 8
♣ A Q J 10 2

He was about to bid two hearts, but as he reached for the bidding box the ten of clubs slipped out of his hand and landed face up on the table.

"Director!" shouted Frawley and Kinston, almost in unison. The Director gave the ruling: West could make any bid, but East was obliged to pass for one round; and if East-West became defenders, the exposed ten of clubs would be a penalty card.

This was the full deal:

Dealer East : North-South vulnerable

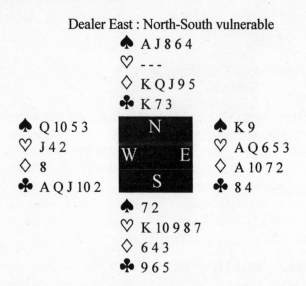

♠ A J 8 6 4
♥ - - -
♦ K Q J 9 5
♣ K 7 3

♠ Q 10 5 3
♥ J 4 2
♦ 8
♣ A Q J 10 2

♠ K 9
♥ A Q 6 5 3
♦ A 10 7 2
♣ 8 4

♠ 7 2
♥ K 10 9 8 7
♦ 6 4 3
♣ 9 6 5

Zettner, downcast at his carelessness, thought for a moment, then bid four hearts: pass, pass, double by Frawley – all pass. The Bridgerama commentator saw only the auction, and had not been apprised of the slip of the card. *"Unlucky break in trumps . . . foreseeable because of North's original double . . . contract probably one or two down."*

Frawley led the seven of spades, aiming to shorten his own trump holding . . . three, pause . . . ace, nine. A spade came back and the king won. The Old Master stopped to think. Frawley was almost certain to have all the missing trumps for the double . . . that was two or three losers . . . the club finesse figured to fail, and the diamonds were a headache. Prospects appeared dim.

The ace of diamonds was cashed and a diamond ruffed. On the queen of spades, declarer discarded a club as South ruffed. A club was returned, and the Old Master proceeded with a cross-ruff: ace of clubs, club ruff, diamond ruff, club ruff to reach this position:

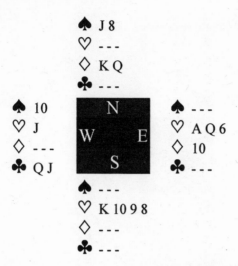

Having lost just two tricks, declarer, East, led the ten of diamonds. If South ruffed high, declarer had three top trumps, and when South ruffed low, the jack over-ruffed. East trumped the next card with the six of hearts, endplaying South.

"Why didn't you duck the first spade?" growled Frawley.

"Several ways to beat the contract . . . Old Master did it just right . . . four hearts doubled was made five times, went off seven times . . . shared top to East-West . . . still trail by just over five tops with six boards to go."

The Old Master glanced at Frawley. A series of errors by the defence. Was that all there was to this game? Capitalize on their mistakes? The age-old question of the perfect hand still haunted him, as he noticed beads of perspiration on Frawley's upper lip.

Then Board 19 arrived:

Dealer South : East-West vulnerable

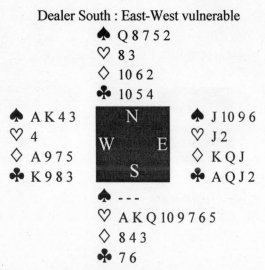

```
                    ♠ Q 8 7 5 2
                    ♥ 8 3
                    ♦ 10 6 2
                    ♣ 10 5 4
   ♠ A K 4 3                        ♠ J 10 9 6
   ♥ 4                              ♥ J 2
   ♦ A 9 7 5                        ♦ K Q J
   ♣ K 9 8 3                        ♣ A Q J 2
                    ♠ - - -
                    ♥ A K Q 10 9 7 6 5
                    ♦ 8 4 3
                    ♣ 7 6
```

Frawley gazed at his eight hearts, tugged nervously at his hair,
then passed. He would catch up later. One club from Zettner,
pass, one spade from the Old Master. Frawley passed again. Three
spades from Zettner, a short pause, and four spades by East. Now
he had them, thought Frawley. Five hearts will be only three off at
worst. This will sound like desperation.

"Five hearts." Pass by Zettner, pass by Kinston. The Old Master
stared at his cards. It seemed obvious to double – two low hearts
and poor trumps. Yet Zettner must be prepared to hear five spades
and Frawley must be prepared to be doubled – he would be too
clever to risk –800. "Five spades." Pass, pass, pass.

*"Twelve pairs played in five hearts doubled for –500. Two East-
Wests were lucky enough to buy it in four spades and made just
ten tricks. One was one off in five spades doubled, losing the
obvious heart, queen of spades and extra spade trick . . . very
clever coup by Frawley . . . fine pass by Kinston, not revealing the
bad break."*

South led the ace of hearts and played a second top heart, ruffed low in dummy. North followed with the ♡8, ♡3. The spade ace revealed the bad break as, Kinston, North, sat back, relaxed.

The Old Master surveyed the possibilities. South apparently started with eight hearts, and no spades. That left five minor suit cards. Could they be just the right way? As he pieced the play together, he felt a long-absent exhilaration. There was a sense of beauty, as well as irony, in the play.

Three rounds of diamonds had to survive. When they did the hand became an open book. Three rounds of clubs followed, finishing in dummy, West, to leave this ending:

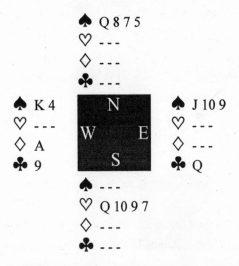

```
              ♠ Q 8 7 5
              ♡ - - -
              ◇ - - -
              ♣ - - -

    ♠ K 4      N       ♠ J 10 9
    ♡ - - -            ♡ - - -
    ◇ A     W     E    ◇ - - -
    ♣ 9        S       ♣ Q

              ♠ - - -
              ♡ Q 10 9 7
              ◇ - - -
              ♣ - - -
```

The Old Master reached across. Savouring the moment, he played the ace of diamonds from dummy. It was pointless for North to ruff with the queen of spades, as East would discard the queen of clubs and would be left with high trumps. So, North ruffed low; East over-ruffed. The club exit was won by North, who now had to play away from the queen of spades.

"Five spades made! Brilliancy at its best . . . still has spark of genius . . . assured of holding on to second position . . ."

The Old Master smiled inwardly. Had the audience seen it, as he had? Did they appreciate that the one sure winner that North held, the queen of spades, had in fact not taken a trick?

Zettner looked rueful, no doubt regretting some of the missed opportunities earlier in the finals. It was too late to worry about that now. The monitor placed Board 20 on the table.

Zettner passed and North-South had a free run:

WEST	NORTH	EAST	SOUTH
Pass	1◇	Pass	2NT
Pass	3◇	Pass	4NT
Pass	5♡	Pass	6NT
Pass	Pass	Pass	

West led the eight of clubs and the Old Master surveyed dummy:

♠ J 6
♡ A Q 6 2
◇ A Q 10 5 4 3
♣ 10

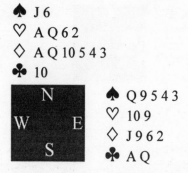

♠ Q 9 5 4 3
♡ 10 9
◇ J 9 6 2
♣ A Q

As declarer, Frawley, was sizing up the slam, the Old Master had his own thoughts. The lead was clearly top-of-nothing; from the cards he could see, it was obvious that Zettner would be hard-pressed to produce a high card. Even though the diamonds were not running, declarer looked to have enough tricks. The Old Master made up his mind quickly, as Frawley called for the ten from dummy.

"The slam is a good one . . ."

Dealer West : Both vulnerable

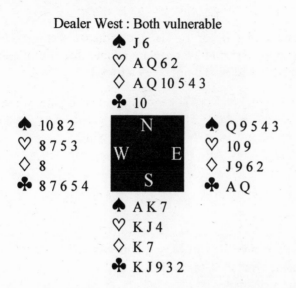

♠ J 6
♡ A Q 6 2
♢ A Q 10 5 4 3
♣ 10

♠ 10 8 2   ♠ Q 9 5 4 3
♡ 8 7 5 3   ♡ 10 9
♢ 8   ♢ J 9 6 2
♣ 8 7 6 5 4   ♣ A Q

♠ A K 7
♡ K J 4
♢ K 7
♣ K J 9 3 2

"The diamonds break badly, but the lucky lie of the clubs is adequate compensation. After East wins the ace of clubs and returns the queen, declarer has twelve top tricks. Nine pairs bid and made 6NT, while the others stopped in 3NT and 4NT. Hello? What's this? East played the queen of clubs at trick one? The strain is obviously starting to tell . . ."

South seized on the queen of clubs as a prize and, seeing thirteen likely tricks, he continued with the king and another diamond. When West showed out, dummy won; the next play took some time. Finally, declarer played a heart to hand and cashed a second heart. Frawley then led the jack of clubs to force out the ace. This was now the position, with the Old Master on lead as East:

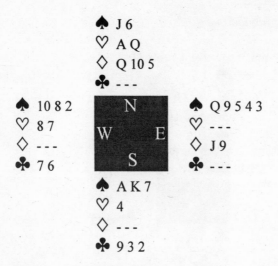

This was the position the Old Master had seen at trick one – he had known then what had to be done. Without further ado he placed the queen of spades on the table and soon entered +100 on his private score-sheet.

"You could have made it," said Kinston.

"I don't want to hear," retorted Frawley.

"Fantastic finish . . . what a card! . . . still not enough to affect the outcome. Four boards left, and the Champions lead by a bit over three tops . . . Old Master back at best after very long absence . . ."

The lights flashed up Board 21:

Dealer North : North-South vulnerable

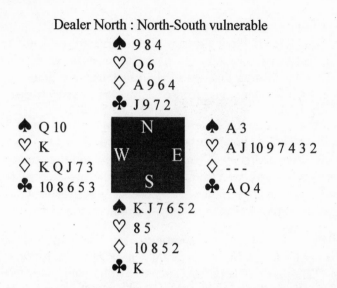

```
                    ♠ 9 8 4
                    ♡ Q 6
                    ♦ A 9 6 4
                    ♣ J 9 7 2
   ♠ Q 10              N              ♠ A 3
   ♡ K                                ♡ A J 10 9 7 4 3 2
   ♦ K Q J 7 3     W       E          ♦ - - -
   ♣ 10 8 6 5 3       S              ♣ A Q 4
                    ♠ K J 7 6 5 2
                    ♡ 8 5
                    ♦ 10 8 5 2
                    ♣ K
```

"Most pairs made eleven tricks in four hearts . . . three managed twelve . . . one made all thirteen, obviously on a spade lead. The two pairs in six hearts received a trump lead and went one down . . . let's see what happens . . ."

The bidding began:

WEST	NORTH	EAST	SOUTH
Zettner	*Kinston*	*Old Master*	*Frawley*
	Pass	1♡	Pass
2♦	Pass	3♡	Pass
4♡	Pass	4♠ . . .	

While Zettner was contemplating what to do over four spades, Frawley had started fidgeting and showing obvious signs of impatience. Finally, he banged his cards on the table and as he did so, the king of clubs flipped up on the table for all to see. Frawley hastened to retrieve it, but the Director was hovering over the table and repeated the ruling of Law 23: North was to pass at his next turn and the king of clubs was a penalty card if North-South became defenders.

While Zettner continued to ponder, memories came flooding back to the Old Master. How Frawley had become President, how Frawley had summoned him for a private meeting, at which he gave the Old Master that dreaded ultimatum: announce your retirement or have your entry refused at all future tournaments.

"How could you do that?" the Old Master had remonstrated, but he knew the answer only too well. The President had the power. He would produce his own 'witnesses' to back up his statements; his committees were well known to follow the presidential line. The Old Master had no choice . . . innocence was irrelevant . . . to fight the ultimatum would bring only discredit on the game.

"Actually, I'll make you a sporting offer," Frawley had said. "Pick a card," he continued, offering a pack of cards to the Old Master. "The term of your 'retirement' will be equivalent to the card you choose." The Old Master had pulled out the ten of hearts, leading to his ten-year retirement.

Zettner finally bid 5♡ and the Old Master pushed on to the small slam.

"Yes, the Old Master has also reached 6 ♡ . The lead will be all important . . . "

With the king of clubs available as a penalty card, the well-known Shakespearian line came to the Old Master: 'If I can catch him once upon the hip, I will feed fat the ancient grudge I bear him.' But was this any way to play bridge? Who would want to win through such a slip, an accident or inadvertence? Better not to win at all than to win that way.

Yet there was the king of clubs as a penalty card and he was looking at the ace and queen in hand. He spoke to the Director: "Is it legitimate for me to waive this penalty card?"

"Certainly," said the Director. "You may permit South to retract the king of clubs, if you wish."

(Repeated for convenience)

Dealer North : North-South vulnerable

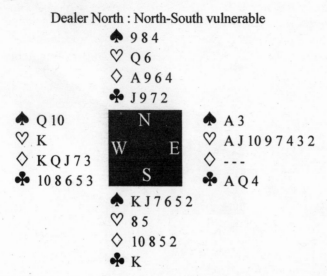

♠ 9 8 4
♡ Q 6
◇ A 9 6 4
♣ J 9 7 2

♠ Q 10
♡ K
◇ K Q J 7 3
♣ 10 8 6 5 3

♠ A 3
♡ A J 10 9 7 4 3 2
◇ - - -
♣ A Q 4

♠ K J 7 6 5 2
♡ 8 5
◇ 10 8 5 2
♣ K

The Old Master looked Frawley in the eye. "Please pick up the king of clubs. Make any lead you wish." Frawley stared back. 'What a fool!' he thought. 'He had me, and he's let me go. He won't win. Winning is everything and winners never give up an edge.'

The Bridgerama commentator was ignorant of the reason for the delay. *"It's taken a long time, but South has led a trump. However, it's not over yet."*

In fact, it was over quite quickly. The Old Master won with the king of hearts and led the king of diamonds, ace, ruff. The ace of hearts drew the remaining trumps and the Old Master exited with the queen of clubs. Frawley won with the king, but he could not escape the endplay to allow an entry to dummy.

"Perhaps if you had let the king of clubs lead stand?" murmured Kinston. Even though Frawley was his partner there was little love lost between them.

"We can all be wise after the event."

"Three boards to go . . . lead whittled down but the Champions still lead by two and a half tops . . . too much to expect a change in the outcome . . . Board 22 is now up . . ."

Dealer East : East-West vulnerable

```
                    ♠ J 9 8 4
                    ♡ A J 6
                    ◇ 5
                    ♣ A J 9 8 2
     ♠ A Q 7            N            ♠ 10
     ♡ 9 8 7 4 2                     ♡ - - -
     ◇ 9 7 4 2     W       E         ◇ A K Q 10 8 6
     ♣ 3              S              ♣ K Q 10 7 6 5
                    ♠ K 6 5 3 2
                    ♡ K Q 10 5 3
                    ◇ J 3
                    ♣ (4)
```

WEST	NORTH	EAST	SOUTH
Zettner	*Kinston*	*Old Master*	*Frawley*
		1◇	2◇*
Pass	4♠	5♣	Pass
5◇	Double	All pass	
*majors			

Four spades doubled was made three times. Five spades doubled was the popular spot, one off. Against the Old Master's five diamonds, Frawley has found the best lead, the king of hearts.

The Old Master ruffed the lead and played the ♠10 to dummy's ace in order to lead a club. Kinston followed with the eight and East's king was ruffed by Frawley. Declarer ruffed the heart exit and cashed the ◇A, drawing the remaining trumps.

As Frawley followed with the ◇J, an oddity caught the Old Master's eye. A second card seemed to be stuck to South's ◇J.

Was it accidental? Was it deliberate? The Old Master decided to leave it for the time being. He continued with a club ruff, heart ruff, club ruff, heart ruff, which left this position:

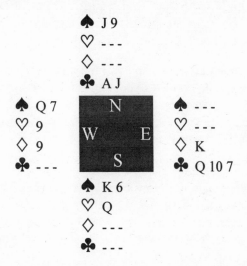

It seemed to the Old Master that he would have to lose two more tricks, as he could make only the remaining trump winners. He reflected on the stuck card, but he wanted to succeed without resorting to the Director. Smiling inwardly, he ruffed a club and ruffed the last heart from dummy. Everyone had two cards except Frawley, who had not noticed, or had not indicated, that he was a card short.

♠ J
♣ A

♠ Q 7   ♠ --
♣ --   ♣ Q 10

♠ K
♣ --

As the Old Master led a club, Frawley suddenly came to life, proclaiming his shortage. The Director was called.

The Director explained: South was obliged to play to this trick, but if he had only 12 cards originally it would be a fouled board. As Frawley played the spade king, the Old Master contemplated the irony of the ending. South had been 'squeezed' out of the ♠K and North had become a stepping-stone to the isolated ♠Q, a winner only because South had ended a card short.

South riffled through his cards, and still the missing card did not appear. Then everyone noticed. The four of clubs had indeed stuck to the jack of diamonds. The Old Master reflected. Should he take the penalty for the revoke? No, making the contract was enough. The mistake seemed to have been genuine. No need to rub it in.

The Old Master wondered. How close was the contest? They were doing sensationally here, but the earlier part of the session had been reasonable, not outstanding. Was there a chance? Dare he hope for a miracle? His ruminations ended as Board 23 appeared:

Dealer South : Both vulnerable

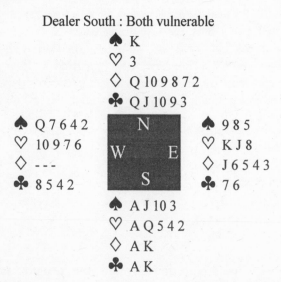

               ♠ K
               ♡ 3
               ◇ Q 10 9 8 7 2
               ♣ Q J 10 9 3

♠ Q 7 6 4 2   ♠ 9 8 5
♡ 10 9 7 6   ♡ K J 8
◇ ---   ◇ J 6 5 4 3
♣ 8 5 4 2   ♣ 7 6

               ♠ A J 10 3
               ♡ A Q 5 4 2
               ◇ A K
               ♣ A K

South	North
2♣	3♦
3♡	4♣
4NT	5♣
5NT	6♦
6NT	Pass

Six no-trumps was the common contract . . . went down three times . . . made ten times . . . two pairs overboard in seven . . . spade lead will spell defeat . . .

Even as the commentator was analysing the deal, a chant had started rippling through the audience. "lead a spade, lead a spade, lead a spade . . ." Zettner, deaf to their prayers, made the safe lead of a heart.

The lead is the ten of hearts . . .

Silence returned to the auditorium.

Declarer should certainly succeed from here . . .

The Old Master played the jack on the ten of hearts; declarer's queen won. The four minor winners were taken. Frawley crossed to the king of spades. Dummy's three club winners followed. The Old Master discarded two spades and, after a brief thought, he pitched the king of hearts on the last club. South discarded a spade and two hearts.

This was the end-position:

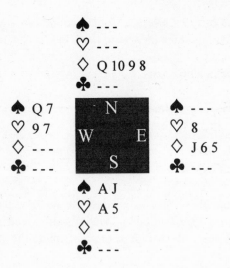

```
                        ♠ - - -
                        ♡ - - -
                        ◇ Q 10 9 8
                        ♣ - - -
    ♠ Q 7          ┌─────────┐        ♠ - - -
    ♡ 9 7          │    N    │        ♡ 8
    ◇ - - -        │  W   E  │        ◇ J 6 5
    ♣ - - -        │    S    │        ♣ - - -
                   └─────────┘
                        ♠ A J
                        ♡ A 5
                        ◇ - - -
                        ♣ - - -
```

*The rest is routine . . . queen and another diamond endplays
East, who has to give the last two tricks either to dummy or to
declarer . . . a two-way stepping-stone . . . the Champions now
have an unassailable lead . . . Yes, the queen of diamonds has
been played . . . next the ten of diamonds . . .*

The Old Master paused. Frawley started drumming his fingers
on the table impatiently, as though wanting to claim. The Old
Master considered the ending. He followed low.

*What's happened? . . . The ten of diamonds has held the trick . . .
next is the nine of diamonds . . . East has taken the jack . . . South
has to make a discard . . . Oh! It's not over yet . . .*

Frawley sat and thought. Seconds turned to minutes. He knew
the Old Master was out to deceive him, but which way? A bead of
perspiration made its way down to his chin. The king of hearts
discard would suggest that East had kept a spade, but that would
be too obvious. So, the Old Master would have a heart left. But
the Old Master would know that he would think this way, so that
the Old Master must really have kept a spade . . .

After a seeming eternity Frawley nervously pulled out a card, put
it back, then tentatively placed an ace on the table. It was red.

He's discarded the ace of hearts . . .

But the rest of the Commentator's words were drowned out in
the cheering. When order returned, Board 24 was on the screen:

*Last board . . . Champions still lead, but what a cliffhanger . . .
only by five match-points . . . exciting hand for East-West . . . Old
Master could actually win it from here . . .*

Dealer West : Nil vulnerable

♠ 10 8 7 6 4
♥ 10 5
♦ 4 3
♣ 9 7 4 3

♠ A K Q J 9   ♠ 5 3 2
♥ A 2   ♥ K Q 9 4
♦ A K 10 9   ♦ Q J 7 6
♣ 6 5   ♣ K J

♠ - - -
♥ J 8 7 6 3
♦ 8 5 2
♣ A Q 10 8 2

*Six spades very unlucky to fail . . . hard to avoid . . . five pairs
went one off in six spades . . . six failed in six no-trumps . . . very
unlucky . . . spades vile . . . clubs both wrong . . . four bid six
diamonds . . . twice by East, making . . . twice by West, made once
on a heart lead, down once on a club lead . . . any positive score
will win it for the Old Master . . . any negative will leave the
Champions in front . . .*

♠ A K Q J 9   ♠ 5 3 2
♡ A 2   ♡ K Q 9 4
◇ A K 10 9   ◇ Q J 7 6
♣ 6 5   ♣ K J

(Repeated for convenience)

Zettner, West, opened two clubs and the Old Master responded two hearts. Two spades from Zettner; the Old Master reviewed the options. He could raise, but three small was no treasure.

'The Italians had the right idea,' he thought, 'Best to have queen third or better for immediate support.'

"Two no-trumps," said the Old Master. 'Can always show spade support later,' he thought.

"Three diamonds," said Zettner.

'What now?' thought the Old Master. 'Back to spades? Raise the diamonds? Game or slam?'

If he bids three no-trumps, it's all over . . if he bids a slam, he will need a lucky lead . . .

"Three no-trumps, three no-trumps, three no-trumps . . .." the unrealistic chant went round the audience.

He has bid four no-trumps and West has replied five spades . . .

The chant immediately changed: "Six diamonds, six diamonds, six diamonds . . ."

Even if he chooses six diamonds, the slam figures to fail . . . a spade lead or a club lead will beat it.

Oblivious to the pandemonium in the auditorium, the Old Master reflected in the silence of the sealed room. 'Partner could hold the ace of clubs or the queen,' he pondered, and yet the king of clubs continued to obsess him. The vision of the perfect hand had long deserted his thoughts.

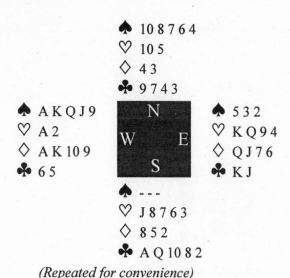

♠ 108764
♡ 10 5
◇ 4 3
♣ 9 7 4 3

♠ A K Q J 9
♡ A 2
◇ A K 10 9
♣ 6 5

♠ 5 3 2
♡ K Q 9 4
◇ Q J 7 6
♣ K J

♠ - - -
♡ J 8 7 6 3
◇ 8 5 2
♣ A Q 10 8 2

(Repeated for convenience)

Finally he made up his mind. "Six no-trumps." The audience groaned. Some started to leave.

Terribly unlucky . . . so near and yet so far . . . still a fantastic effort to get so close . . .

Frawley, South, led a diamond, won in dummy. The Old Master felt the hand was an anti-climax. 'Twelve easy tricks,' he thought, as he cashed a spade at trick two. Frawley's club discard brought him up short. 'Serves me right,' he ruefully chided himself. 'The game is always greater than the player. Now what?'

It looked as though he would have to guess the clubs or hope for a discarding error. Was that the essence of the game, to hope for a mistake or make a lucky guess? There had to be more. He glanced briefly at Frawley. Despite the previous boards, Frawley was very relaxed. In a flash, the Old Master knew . . . the clubs were both wrong . . . but then, what chance was there?

The Old Master is just delaying the inevitable . . . will have to tackle the clubs sooner or later . . . South can then claim . . .

On the remaining diamonds, Kinston threw two clubs and Frawley let go another club. With the lead in dummy, declarer played off two more spade winners, arriving at this ending:

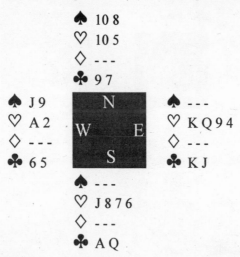

♠ 10 8
♡ 10 5
◊ - - -
♣ 9 7

♠ J 9
♡ A 2
◊ - - -
♣ 6 5

♠ - - -
♡ K Q 9 4
◊ - - -
♣ K J

♠ - - -
♡ J 8 7 6
◊ - - -
♣ A Q

I don't believe it . . . can it be? . . . he's cashed the jack of spades and discarded the jack of clubs . . . South has to keep the hearts and has been forced to throw the club queen . . .

A complete hush had settled on the audience as the Old Master's plan became evident. He pieced the play together once more, as he had from the moment he realized the club position; a sense of relief swept through the Old Master. This was what the game was truly about. It was not a game of error, not a matter of profiting through the lapse of an opponent, not winning at all costs by technical adherence to the Laws. There was an innate beauty in being set a challenge, with everything apparently wrong, yet to come out on top, to conquer adversity just by one's wits. This world had a magic of its own. How dull of him to think that the spades would divide! Then this deal would have meant nothing.

The Old Master played the ace of hearts, then a heart to his king. No wonder he had been obsessed with the king of clubs during the bidding. It had been the key to the whole hand.

Treasuring the moment, he pulled the king of clubs from his hand and, as a tear trickled slowly down his face, he placed it face up on the table, with just one word.

"Checkmate."

Last Chance

© Bridge World Magazine Inc.1994 (March issue)

Only six boards to go . . . the Bridgerama commentator's voice boomed through the packed auditorium . . . *Champions 51 imps in front . . . Challengers fought well . . even the Old Master cannot save them from here . . . Bermuda Bowl effectively over . . .*

The Old Master stared down at his cards. Six boards left. They had scarcely made any headway in the first ten boards of this final session. 50 imps down at the start, probably about the same now. Not much hope and the Champions were already sitting back with confidence.

Still, it had been a good fight. No one had given them *any* chance. And he *had* been out of the game for over ten years. There was no shame in running second. Still . . . He took his cards from the board. He was the dealer. He looked at :

♠ J 7   ♡ K 5 2   ◇ A 4 2   ♣ A Q J 9 5

He placed the 1NT card down and pushed the bidding tray under the screen. He recalled when he had learnt the game originally. Back then I would not have opened 1NT with such spades, he thought. How times have changed.

The tray came back. 2♠ on his left, 3NT from partner. The bidding ended. The screen was raised a fraction as the 5 of spades opening lead was made and the Old Master surveyed the dummy :

♠ Q 9 3
♡ A Q 10
◇ J 6 5
♣ 6 4 3 2

♠ J 7
♡ K 5 2
◇ A 4 2
♣ A Q J 9 5

'Nothing timid about my young partner,' he thought. He played low from dummy on the ♠5 lead and East's 10 of spades was taken by the jack.

'Clearly the club finesse needs to be on,' thought the Old Master as he contemplated his next play.

In the Closed Room 3NT was reached without any interference the commentator told the audience who could see the whole deal:

Dealer South : Nil vulnerable

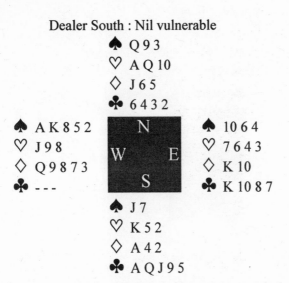

♠ Q 9 3
♡ A Q 10
♢ J 6 5
♣ 6 4 3 2

♠ A K 8 5 2
♡ J 9 8
♢ Q 9 8 7 3
♣ - - -

♠ 10 6 4
♡ 7 6 4 3
♢ K 10
♣ K 10 8 7

♠ J 7
♡ K 5 2
♢ A 4 2
♣ A Q J 9 5

West led the five of spades . . . South won the jack . . . a heart to the ace was followed by the club finesse . . . bad break meant almost certain defeat . . . South led a low heart . . . West found the fine play of inserting the jack of hearts . . . now South could not score five club tricks . . . contract went one down . . . play here will go the same way . . . I have no doubt West will also find the jack of hearts play . . . unless the Old Master can see through the cards and the screens . . . (a titter ran through the audience) . . . *there will be no swing . . .*

'Play for the contract or play for overtricks,' thought the Old Master. The sanctity of the contract. That's why he loved teams. The distortion of pairs irked him. 'If the clubs behave I have ten tricks, but what if there is a bad break?' The Old Master saw the solution in an instant. At trick two he led the ♡K and overtook it with dummy's ace. A club to the queen held the trick and the bad break was revealed. A low heart was led and the 10 of hearts finessed. When that held, the Old Master claimed nine tricks.

Brilliant safety play . . . 10 years have not dimmed the spark . . . 10 imps to the Challengers . . . they trail by 41.

The screen went blank. Then the next deal appeared:

Dealer West : North-South vulnerable

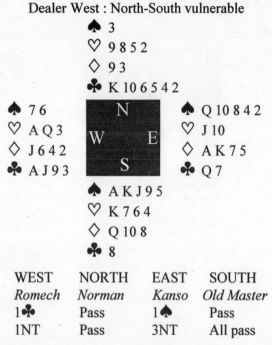

```
                    ♠ 3
                    ♡ 9 8 5 2
                    ◇ 9 3
                    ♣ K 10 6 5 4 2
  ♠ 7 6                             ♠ Q 10 8 4 2
  ♡ A Q 3          N                ♡ J 10
  ◇ J 6 4 2    W       E            ◇ A K 7 5
  ♣ A J 9 3         S                ♣ Q 7
                    ♠ A K J 9 5
                    ♡ K 7 6 4
                    ◇ Q 10 8
                    ♣ 8
```

WEST	NORTH	EAST	SOUTH
Romech	*Norman*	*Kanso*	*Old Master*
1♣	Pass	1♠	Pass
1NT	Pass	3NT	All pass

When East bid 1♠, the Old Master wondered whether he should double 3NT for a spade lead. Partner might have only one spade and even then a spade lead might not defeat 3NT. He made up his mind. Over 3NT he passed without pause. As the Old Master expected, North produced the club lead: five – seven – eight – nine. West returned the three of clubs and North took the king. The Old Master discarded the four of hearts.

After a moment's thought, David Norman, only 22 and in his first world championship although he had been playing for eight years, switched to the three of spades : two from dummy and the Old Master won with the nine. When the king of spades was cashed, North discarded a club.

What now? wondered the Old Master.

*. . . same contract in other room . . . same early play . . . South
exited with a heart, ducked to dummy's jack . . . repeated the heart
finesse and cashed the clubs and the ♡A . . . down to four cards,
South kept ♠A and ♢Q108 but declarer crossed to the ♢A and
led the spade, endplaying South . . . 3NT made . . . not a difficult
play at this level . . . West is sure to find the winning line . . .*

Before the commentator could finish a roar went up from the
audience. The Old Master had placed the ♡K on the table. West
struggled, but with the hearts blocked there were only eight tricks.

*Another 10 imps to the Challengers . . . down 31 imps with 4
boards left . . . no doubt about the Old Master . . .*

The lights flickered as the next deal appeared on the screen :

Dealer North : Both vulnerable

```
                    ♠ 10 9 6
                    ♡ 8 5 4
                    ♢ 6 3
                    ♣ A J 10 5 4
   ♠ K 9 3            N          ♠ 7 5 4 2
   ♡ K 9 2                       ♡ J 7 6 3
   ♢ K J 10 9 4    W     E       ♢ Q 8
   ♣ 7 2              S          ♣ 9 8 6
                    ♠ A Q J
                    ♡ A Q 10
                    ♢ A 7 5 2
                    ♣ K Q 3
```

*In the closed room the Champions played in 3NT from the South
seat . . . West led diamonds . . . South won the third round . . .
cashed five clubs . . . West discarded a spade and two hearts . . .
declarer mispicked and took the heart finesse for one down . . .
the Old Master will certainly be in 3NT . . . can he pick finesses
better than the champions? . . .*

The bidding was over swiftly. The Old Master opened 2NT in third seat and North raised to 3NT. West led the jack of diamonds and East played the queen. The Old Master ducked. He ducked the next diamond and won the third round. With barely a pause he continued with the king and queen of clubs and then exited with a diamond. West won and cashed his last diamond on which the Old Master threw a heart. The forced major return gave the Old Master his ninth trick.

. . . routine endplay by the Old Master . . . silly declarer mistake in the closed room . . . 12 more imps to the Challengers . . . they trail by 19 . . . three boards to go . . . next board features a great result by the young Challengers . . . just take a look at this . . .

Dealer East : Nil vulnerable

```
            ♠ 10 8 7 2
            ♡ J 9 8 2
            ◇ 2
            ♣ J 10 8 7
♠ 9 5 4         N          ♠ A K
♡ Q 7                      ♡ A K 4 3
◇ K 9 7 5    W     E       ◇ A J 6
♣ Q 9 3 2         S        ♣ A K 5 4
            ♠ Q J 6 3
            ♡ 10 6 5
            ◇ Q 10 8 4 3
            ♣ 6
```

In the closed room East opened 2♣ and after 2◇ by West, East jumped to 3NT showing 25+ . . . West bid 5NT asking East to pick a slam either in a minor or in no-trumps . . . East bid 6♣ and played it there . . . just watch this play, ladies and gentlemen . . . The five of hearts was led and it seems as though East must lose a trump trick and the diamond finesse as well . . . look what happened . . .

As the commentator called each card played, the light behind that card went out.

The heart queen won and declarer cashed ace-king of clubs . . . bad news . . . now hearts were continued and dummy ruffed the fourth round with the 9 of clubs . . . the king of diamonds was cashed and a second diamond led . . . if North ruffed, that was the end of the defence, so North discarded a spade . . . you can see the end-position after declarer has won with the ace of diamonds.

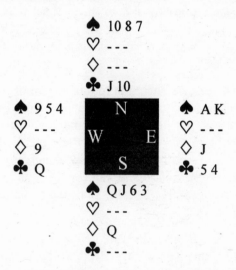

♠ 10 8 7
♡ - - -
◇ - - -
♣ J 10

♠ 9 5 4   ♠ A K
♡ - - -   ♡ - - -
◇ 9   ◇ J
♣ Q   ♣ 5 4

♠ Q J 6 3
♡ - - -
◇ Q
♣ - - -

Declarer cashed the ace and king of spades, played a club to the queen and ruffed a spade in hand . . . both North and South were able to win the thirteenth trick . . . very, very pretty . . . can the Champions match that? . . . Let's see . . .

The Old Master waited until the recorder told them they could proceed. The audience was being told what had already occurred. The last few boards had been good. Were they pickups or pushes? Was there a hope or was the match over?

Suddenly a wave of tiredness swept through the Old Master. He could feel it through his bones. No, it was not the tournament, although fourteen days had elapsed since it all began. Ten years ago he had won the world crown and then left the bridge world. No, he did not regret it, but he had missed it. His family needed him. They were a wonderful ten years, partly spent with his married daughter and son-in-law and as much time as possible with his grandchildren. He loved them all so much. Although twinges occurred, he would not have exchanged those family-filled years for anything.

And then came that surprise invitation to join a team of rookies. Well, not really rookies, but they were all so young. They had had their national successes, but nothing on the international scene. And they had invited him, old enough to be their grandfather, to join them. He had mentioned it as a joke to his daughter and she had urged him to accept it. And he did, not expecting they would qualify to play for their country. Yet they had. And then they won their zonal play-off as well.

The youngsters were full of vitality and unbounded enthusiasm. It reminded him of his own young days. And now here they were, three boards from the end of the world championship. It had been a long haul. The years were exacting their toll. He fended the tiredness off as he would an old enemy.

The recorder's voice broke his reverie. "Please start."

East-West had a complex auction, which the Old Master could follow on his system pack. He remembered the old system cards method. How archaic that all seemed now. Each pair now had to submit a disk with their complete system on it. The Old Master punched each bid as it was made to find out its meaning.

Dealer East : Nil vulnerable

♠ 10 8 7 2
♡ J 9 8 2
◇ 2
♣ J 10 8 7

♠ 9 5 4
♡ Q 7
◇ K 9 7 5
♣ Q 9 3 2

♠ A K
♡ A K 4 3
◇ A J 6
♣ A K 5 4

♠ Q J 6 3
♡ 10 6 5
◇ Q 10 8 4 3
♣ 6

(Repeated for convenience)

WEST	EAST	
	1♣	- - - artificial and forcing
1◇ (1)	2♣	- - - artificial, 23+ points
2NT (2)	3♣	- - - artificial enquiry
3♡ (3)	4♣	- - - RKCB based on clubs
4♡ (4)	5◇	- - - asking bid in diamonds
5♠ (5)	6NT	
Pass		

(1) Artificial, negative
(2) 6-9 balanced, no major
(3) Exactly 3-2-4-4 pattern
(4) ♣Q held but no key cards
(5) ◇K but no ◇Q

   North fidgeted with his lead. Everything seemed dangerous. The asking bid in diamonds suggested that diamonds might be a weak spot and the two of diamonds appeared.

Dealer East : Nil vulnerable

♠ 10 8 7 2
♡ J 9 8 2
◇ 2
♣ J 10 8 7

♠ 9 5 4
♡ Q 7
◇ K 9 7 5
♣ Q 9 3 2

♠ A K
♡ A K 4 3
◇ A J 6
♣ A K 5 4

♠ Q J 6 3
♡ 10 6 5
◇ Q 10 8 4 3
♣ 6

After the diamond two lead Romech called for the six from dummy, the Old Master played the ten and the king won. As Romech continued with a diamond and North discarded a spade, the commentator broke into an excited jabber.

West can set up three diamond tricks . . . after he takes the ace of diamonds and plays the diamond jack next, South wins the queen and declarer can now squeeze North . . . even a diamond back does not help the defence . . . a club is discarded from dummy, followed by three rounds of clubs, ending in hand . . . the fourth diamond will squeeze North . . . champions are about to pick up 2 imps to seal their victory . . .

Romech thwarted the commentators, as players are wont to do, by playing the jack of diamonds from dummy.

. . . the result will be the same . . . after the queen of diamonds wins, the same squeeze will operate . . .

The Old Master was thinking. West was almost sure to have the missing queens to justify the 2NT rebid and North must have precarious holdings to start with that singleton diamond. The Old Master went over the play of the next few tricks.

No, there was no way that North could avoid the squeeze. The fourth diamond winner would do its damage. There was no way for Romech to misplay it.

Then he saw it. What if there was no fourth diamond winner? The Old Master pushed the queen of diamonds, half-jutting out of his hand, back in line with his other cards. A bemused smile lit up his face as he remembered his old partner's regular admonition, "Take your tricks, that's all you gotta do, take your tricks." What would he think of this play? He played the four of diamonds under the jack.

A collective gasp went up from the audience.

He's refused the diamond trick. He's mad. He's lost his senses. No, it's a brilliancy.

Romech cashed the ace and king of clubs. The Old Master threw a spade. Next came the top spades and another club but there were eleven tricks there and only eleven.

Unbelievable, ladies and gentlemen . . . I have seen it and I still can't believe it . . . I cannot remember a better card anytime in any world championship . . . that's one down in 6NT and 50 to the Challengers . . . 14 imps brings the score down to a difference of only just five . . . the Champions lead by 5 imps with two boards to play . . . do we have a boilover? . . . No, the next board will see the Champions well in front again . . . look what happened to the Challengers . . .

214 Right Through the Pack Again

Dealer South : North-South vulnerable

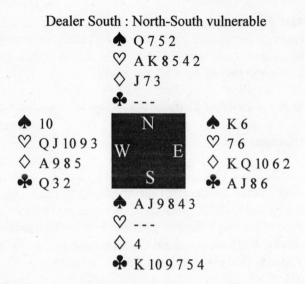

♠ Q 7 5 2
♡ A K 8 5 4 2
♢ J 7 3
♣ - - -

♠ 10
♡ Q J 10 9 3
♢ A 9 8 5
♣ Q 3 2

♠ K 6
♡ 7 6
♢ K Q 10 6 2
♣ A J 8 6

♠ A J 9 8 4 3
♡ - - -
♢ 4
♣ K 10 9 7 5 4

*In the Closed Room the Champions bid to the poor 6♠ . . .
hopeless contract . . . East-West took the phantom in 7♢ . . .
inexperience of youth . . . doubled of course . . . the defence was
merciless . . . South led the four of clubs, suit preference for
hearts and North ruffed . . . top heart cashed then a low heart
ruffed . . . ten of clubs returned and ruffed . . . spade to the ace
and another club ruff . . . Champions made tricks with each of
their trumps . . . top class defence . . . +1400 . . . worthy
champions . . .*

The Old Master stared at his black 6-6. How to bid this
collection? The new school had methods to deal with these. He
could never come to grips with their never-ending artificialities.
Where had the fun and the adventure gone? Only eight points, but
the suits were strong. Had he been dealt these cards as a test? Was
there any hope? Was this the last chance? He opened 1♠.

The bidding appeared quickly on the Bridgerama screen:

WEST	NORTH	EAST	SOUTH
Romech	*Norman*	*Kanso*	*Old Master*
			1♠
2♡	4♣	4♢	4NT
6♢	Pass	Pass	6♠
Pass	Pass	Double	All pass

4♣ was explained as a splinter, short in clubs and good spade support. As soon as the Old Master heard that, he was determined to bid the slam. He decided to use 4NT to try to muddy the waters.

Sensible double by East . . . silly to be pushed into a sacrifice just because of the vulnerability . . . should be 17 or 18 imps to the Champions . . . West will surely lead the ace of diamonds . . .

The audience was already ahead of the commentator and the chant started slowly and then surged around the room '. . . Lead a heart, lead a heart, lead a heart . . .'

The screen flickered. The lead appeared. It was the ace of diamonds. A numb silence settled over the auditorium, as at a funeral. The spectators resumed their seats.

West continued with a second diamond and the Old Master ruffed. 'East figures to have the king of spades,' he thought. 'He could not count on a club trick and any more than one trick from partner, so where is the double otherwise? Anyway, the play has to be a crossruff.'

The play continued with a club ruff, heart ruff, club ruff, heart ruff, club ruff. Then came the top hearts. East could not afford to throw the ace of clubs. The Old Master could then simply draw trumps via a finesse. Ruffing the heart would also do East no good, so he discarded diamonds. This was the end-position on view in the Bridgerama room:

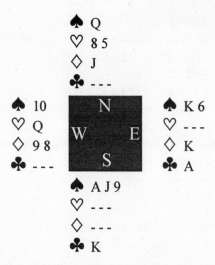

```
              ♠ Q
              ♡ 8 5
              ◇ J
              ♣ - - -
  ♠ 10                    ♠ K 6
  ♡ Q        N            ♡ - - -
  ◇ 9 8    W   E          ◇ K
  ♣ - - -     S           ♣ A
              ♠ A J 9
              ♡ - - -
              ◇ - - -
              ♣ K
```

The Old Master savoured the ending. How remarkable this game is, he pondered. An opening bid on the slenderest of values, pushing on to a slam with such a modest count even after partner's splinter indicated wastage in clubs, bidding Blackwood when holding a void, breaching almost every rule and still the cards allowed him to succeed. The prize was there. He had but to grasp it.

He called for dummy's diamond, ruffed it in hand and the king of clubs was ruffed in dummy. When the heart was led from dummy at trick 12, East conceded.

The auditorium erupted. Shouting, cheering, stamping, clapping. It took minutes to restore order.

What more can be said . . . snatched victory out of defeat . . . Challengers score +1660 and 6 imps . . . the Old Master proved the sacrifice right in the other room . . . the Challengers lead by one imp . . . one board to play . . . can we please have some quiet . . .

The clamour subsided to a constant buzz as the final deal was revealed.

The Old Master studied his cards. :

    ♠ A K 8 6 4
    ♡ A
    ◇ A Q J 9 8 2
    ♣ 4

West was the dealer. East-West were vulnerable. When the bidding board came to the Master, it revealed :

WEST	NORTH	EAST	SOUTH
Romech	*Norman*	*Kanso*	*Old Master*
4♡	Pass	Pass	?

'What a way to finish,' he thought. 'Anything could be right. We might have a grand slam. There might be no more than a game. Double is possible, so is 5♡. Even 5◇ might work out. Still, West is vulnerable against not. It won't be a weak pre-empt. Let's play for a positive score.'

The Old Master selected the 4♠ card and the bidding passed below the screen.

When the tray returned, West and North had passed. Kanso had selected the 5♡ card and the closed circuit TV revealed the Old Master contemplating his next action.

In the other room, 5 ♡ was doubled . . . the commentator told the audience . . . this had to fail by one trick . . . +200 to the Champions . . . if this result is duplicated, the Challengers will win by 1 imp . . . the South hand is very difficult . . .

The audience took up the cue. 'Double, double, double'. The Old Master doubled. Wild cheering. The bidding went back under the screen. West passed and Norman, North, started thinking.

"What is he thinking about?" . . . "He has to pass." . . . "Don't
worry, he will pass." The chant resumed, "Pass, Pass, Pass, Pass."
The TV monitors revealed Norman with his head in his hands. He
was almost shaking.

*Be fair . . . he has a serious problem . . . if he passes, it is all
over . . . if he bids . . .*

The commentator was interrupted by a universal groan. The
screen revealed that North had bid 5♠. Everyone passed and the
audience awaited the opening lead.

At the table, the Old Master knew his young partner's problem.
While West was considering the opening lead, the Old Master
said softly, "Don't worry. I'm sure you made the right decision."
When the screen was raised, the Old Master saw :

> NORTH
> ♠ 10 9 7 3 2
> ♡ 2
> ◇ 5 3
> ♣ K Q J 10 9
>
> SOUTH
> ♠ A K 8 6 4
> ♡ A
> ◇ A Q J 9 8 2
> ♣ 4

The six of clubs was led and East took the ace. After a brief
thought East returned the eight of clubs and the Old Master
considered his play.

Meanwhile in the auditorium, the commentator, with the benefit
of seeing all four hands, was analysing the outcome while West
was considering his lead. All eyes were glued to the screen.

Dealer West : East-West vulnerable

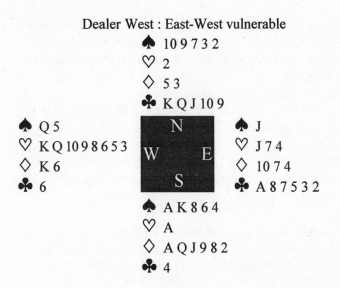

♠ 10 9 7 3 2
♡ 2
◇ 5 3
♣ K Q J 10 9

♠ Q 5
♡ K Q 10 9 8 6 5 3
◇ K 6
♣ 6

♠ J
♡ J 7 4
◇ 10 7 4
♣ A 8 7 5 3 2

♠ A K 8 6 4
♡ A
◇ A Q J 9 8 2
♣ 4

. . . if South had doubled 4 ♡ and North had bid the spades first, 5 ♠ would likely have made . . . East would probably not lead the ace of clubs and on any other lead, eleven tricks are easy . . . with West on lead, a club lead is much more likely . . . on a heart lead, South will make, but on a club lead, East can return a club and that will create a trump trick for the defence . . .

South will then lose one club, one spade and when the diamond finesse loses, South will go one down . . .

Yes, West has led a club and it is all over . . . one down gives the Champions +50 and 6 imps . . . a lucky let off for the Champions . . . they will win by 5 imps . . . bad luck for the Challengers . . . so near and yet so far . . .

No one had moved from their seats. Having seen so many brilliancies, they expected the Old Master to produce one more. Their eyes told them that the contract had to fail, their hearts wished for a miracle.

At the table the Old Master focussed on the club return. West had bid hearts, East had supported. Yet West had led a club. Surely a singleton. And East had returned a club, not a heart. Confirmation that the lead was a singleton. Even if this trick were lost, the diamond finesse would probably work.

Still he did not play. What was the trump layout? If the lead was a singleton, West would not also have a singleton trump. Two singletons were unlikely and to lead a singleton with only one trump was even less likely. Then the Old Master saw what he had missed. If West had two spades, there was no problem.

The Old Master ruffed the club return with the ace of spades, cashed the king of spades to which all followed and then cashed the ace of hearts. The audience saw this end-position :

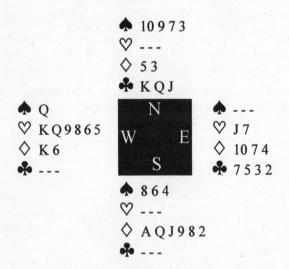

```
                    ♠ 10 9 7 3
                    ♡ - - -
                    ◇ 5 3
                    ♣ K Q J
   ♠ Q                                ♠ - - -
   ♡ K Q 9 8 6 5        N             ♡ J 7
   ◇ K 6            W       E         ◇ 10 7 4
   ♣ - - -              S             ♣ 7 5 3 2
                    ♠ 8 6 4
                    ♡ - - -
                    ◇ A Q J 9 8 2
                    ♣ - - -
```

The Old Master played the 4 of spades and as West revealed the queen, the Old Master said just one word,

"Checkmate."

Appendix 2 : Source of deals

Other than the constructed deals, this is where they arose.

Card	Page	Source
♣2	142	Constructed
♣3	162	2006 Commonwealth Nations Championships
♣4	160	Constructed
♣5	96	Constructed
♣6	88	Rubber bridge deal (reported by Seamus Browne)
♣7	71	2004 North American Spring Nationals
♣8	90	From OKbridge, reported by Pamela Granovetter
♣9	78	2004 World Open Teams Olympiad, Istanbul
♣9 #2	80	Lebhar IMP Pairs, USA Nationals. West: Mike Flader
♣10	108	From the final of a national teams championship
♣J	49	World Youth Championships: Oliver Burgess led the ♣J and declarer went one down in 7♠.
♣Q	110	From the final of a national teams event
♣Q #2	112	Played by Tim Seres, rubber bridge, 2006
♣K	128	Selection for national representative team 2005
♣A	92	Selection for a National Teams Championship
♣A #2	94	Selection for a National Teams Championship
◇2	140	2005 national teams. Declarer: Edward Griffin
◇3	63	Diana Smart in *The Bridge World*, December, 2002.
◇4	147	Based on a deal created by Martin Hoffman
◇5	86	Constructed
◇6	130	2003 Bermuda Bowl match, USA1 vs USA2
◇7	69	2002 McConnell Cup semi-finals
◇7 #2	70	2002 McConnell Cup semi-finals
◇8	138	Based on a deal from a national Swiss pairs event
◇9	102	National Teams Championship, 2005
◇10	156	Based on a deal supplied by Richard Oshlag, USA
◇10 #2	158	Constructed
◇J	152	National Teams Championship. East: Tim Seres
◇Q	136	Constructed
◇K	46	Constructed
◇A	114	Constructed
◇A #2	115	Australian National Butler Trials, 2003

♥2	74	Vanderbilt final, USA, 2005. East: Mike Becker
♥3	145	2007 national teams. Declarer: Joachim Haffer
♥4	105	Constructed
♥5	106	2005 Pacific Asian Open Teams
♥6	131	Constructed
♥7	84	From Tim Seres, rubber bridge, 2002
♥8	56	Australian National Butler Trials 2005
♥8 #2	60	Constructed by Tim Bourke
♥9	76	Italy vs USA. Giorgio Belladonna, West, returned a heart at trick 4 and declarer escaped for two down.
♥10	122	1979 club duplicate in New Zealand
♥10 #2	124	Constructed
♥J	98	2005 national teams selection tournament
♥J #2	100	2003 Bermuda Bowl and Venice Cup semi-finals
♥Q	164	Constructed
♥K	148	2005 national selection. West: Matthew McManus
♥A	66	2004 Yeh Bros Cup, held in Beijing.
♥A #2	67	2004 Yeh Bros Cup, held in Beijing.
♠2	166	2008 New Year Teams, Sydney
♠3	126	2004 national teams event
♠4	40	2002 European Open Teams. Successful defenders were Tomasz Gotard and Kosef PieKarek
♠5	82	2007 Lederer Memorial Trophy. Gunnar Hallberg – Andrew McIntosh won Best Defended Hand prize.
♠6	104	2005 Pacific Asian Open Teams
♠6 #2	120	Teams match, Santa Fe, December 25, 2007
♠7	62	Constructed by Tim Bourke
♠8	54	Australian National Butler Trials, 2005
♠8 #2	58	Selection for a National Teams Championship
♠9	42	2005 Pacific Asian Open Teams
♠9 #2	44	Constructed
♠10	154	Based on a hand played by Steen Moller, Denmark
♠J	50	Played by Bill Root in the 1967 Bermuda Bowl
♠J #2	53	From Tim Seres, rubber bridge, 2005
♣Q	133	Constructed
♣Q #2	134	2005 national teams event
♣K	150	2005 national teams selection
♣A	116	2005 Australian National Butler Trials
♣A #2	117	2005 Australian National Butler Trials